BURNOUT DIARIES:
How Work Stress Almost Killed Me

By Janna Donovan

Copyright © 2021 Wydie Press LLC

All rights reserved. No part of this publication may be reproduced, distributed, or transmitted in any form or by any means, including photocopying, recording, or other electronic or mechanical methods, without the prior written permission of the publisher, except in the case of brief quotations embodied in critical reviews and certain other non-commercial uses permitted by copyright law.

ISBN: 978-1-7375765-1-8

Editing by Dustin Bilyk @ The Author's Hand
Front cover and jacket design by Ianskey @ 99Designs
Author photograph by Coral Abood

Printed by Kindle Direct Publishing in the United States of America. First printing edition 2021.

Visit: http://www.workstress.guru

THE HOLY BIBLE, NEW INTERNATIONAL VERSION®, NIV® Copyright © 1973, 1978, 1984, 2011 by Biblica, Inc.™ Used by permission. All rights reserved worldwide.

Pseudonyms and composites have been used to protect the privacy of actors in the story. Some dates are approximations.

This book is dedicated to Mom, Dave, Sean and Tara.
Because of you, I lived to tell about it.

Contents

Introduction 9

Chapter 1: How Did I Get Here?... 13

Chapter 2: Don't Wannabe a Wannabe 35

Chapter 3: A Baby Elephant and the Decision to Fight 46

Chapter 4: It's Time to Do Something 56

Chapter 5: August in the Red 64

Chapter 6: Independence from What? 78

Chapter 7: Depression Comes 87

Chapter 8: Holding on Tight 102

Chapter 9: Don't Be Afraid of Anybody 109

Chapter 10: Games People Play 122

Chapter 11: The Big Day 133

Chapter 12: Langkawi 149

Chapter 13: 'Til the Bitter End 160

Chapter 14: Dignity, In an Exit Interview? 168

Chapter 15: It's Finally Over: Now What? 173

Chapter 16: Will and Desire to Change 187

Chapter 17: The Boy's Got No Fear 195

Chapter 18: Party Time! 217

Chapter 19: Bangkok then Back to the Beginning 226

Chapter 20: A Letter to Myself 235

The Secrets to Thriving: Lies, Habits & Changes 240

Foreword

Janna is one of those people you meet and you know there is so much more to her than you see. As someone who plays a small role in the events of this truthful story, I can recall with vividness the events she describes. I can see myself in my side of the story, which is never the whole story.

At some point in her story, I left Penang, Malaysia, and continued in the direction of working with humans in service of their flourishing. Strangely enough, that led to me navigating through my own heroic leadership, PTSD, and burnout. Listening to Janna's voice as I read her words, I am once again moved by her courage and commitment. I was always impressed by her openness, curiosity, and determination. I am delighted she has created this honest and graphic work of heart that will give readers the opportunity to develop awareness and increase their resourcefulness. As I continue to work with and help leaders, teams, and professionals today, the very real experiences described by Janna continue to play out with increasing intensity.

If you have this book in your hands, don't let the opportunity go. Take what's for you. Connect where you connect. And let Janna's candor and compassion empower you to make choices in service of your well-being, genuine success, and happiness.

Craig McKenzie
Director, Coach Educator, Supervisor

Acknowledgements

Whenever I read my favorite authors, I always notice how long the acknowledgements section is. The gratitude continues through a very long list of people, and I am amazed that writing a book requires so many eyes and so much care from so many people.

Now that I've finished telling this story, I too am amazed at how many people I wish to—no, that I *need to*—thank. My only hesitation in thanking people in print is that I might forget a person who has been crucial to the process, and that will not make me, or them, very happy! But I am willing to take that risk in order to permanently record who has been a part of this process.

David, thank you for living through it with me and allowing the most private parts of our lives to be revealed. Sean, thank you so much for being the Intrepid One and embracing your time in Malaysia, even as a young man in grade school.

Mom, Jim, and John, thank you for being such incredible protectors and allowing me to take risks all my life. I am sorry for how much I frightened you, and I am so thankful for the great times we've had back in the U.S.

Tara, the dedication page says it all. You saved my life when I was cracking apart. Thank you so much for your wisdom, love, and humor, as well as the finesse you showed in keeping my family members together. You are truly a powerful woman and a friend beyond compare.

Dustin, the editor who gave this story a chance of becoming a book, thank you from the bottom of my heart.

Your wit, decisiveness, hard work, and positive coaching style provided the perfect blend of creative respect and accountability that I needed to finish.

Darrell, thank you for being the steadiest human around. Thank you for reading my early manuscript and encouraging me to keep writing. Your praise meant so much coming from a man who reads a book a day!

Matthew, Tara, Jenna, and Kim, your emotional reaction to the story, and then your collective statement that this must be published, gave me mountains of certainty when I was not sure.

Susan, who I met in a writer's forum, thank you so much for your consistency, enthusiasm, and beautiful smile. You truly helped me to believe I could make something worth reading.

Thank you, Cathy Fyock, for the community and the advice and the many books you have written to help budding authors.

To everyone who read part or all of the story, thank you so very much for the respect I felt because of how much time and energy you gave: Matthew, Mary, Terry, Dan, Tara, Jenna, Susan, Jordan, Clelland, Spencer, Allen, Tammy, Kim, Mollie, Caroline, Jessica, another Kim and another Tara, and the several people whose names remain private as a part of the story.

And thank you to the counselors, mentors, pastors, and everyone else who helped me heal.

Finally, thank you God for rescuing me with your life, love, Spirit and Son, Jesus.

INTRODUCTION

When we burn out at work, we are afraid to tell our bosses, partners, and colleagues that we are dying inside. We believe it will make things worse. We become secretive, and the things we do to survive work stress are hidden from others. This forces each of us to learn how to survive it on our own. But no one should have to do it alone.

I wrote this book to show how we survive tough times and dark periods brought on by work—to explain my experience, my thoughts, and my opinions as I became burnt out and depressed. It is meant to give voice to something other than blame or raging against the corporate world. It's about personal responsibility and individual healing.

This book goes much deeper into my life than I ever planned. I was ashamed that you would see my desperation, my hidden fear that I was cracking apart, and the doubts I had about whether I would even survive the experience.

As I look back over this time in my life, I remember that, while others were doing very well at the company, I lived with constant dread and the inability to sleep or even think straight. Nothing I did to make it go away was ever enough.

After several months of wishing I had a way out, I recall lying on the hard floor in the middle of the night, entertaining the thought of jumping off the 23rd floor balcony. A chilling fear runs through me when I remember how much I argued with everyone who tried to help, from family members to doctors. I even argued with them when I was considering ending my life.

When I began writing, I put these memories aside because I was certain it would be too hard to read. I thought to myself, 'Too dark. No one wants to hear your negative, whiny crap! They need you to stay positive, to get through the chaos and, above all, they need solutions. Be solution-focused!' So, I wrote about research results, better habits, and life hacks, many of which you may already know.

My 130-page diary was only supposed to be referenced. The real book was being written to "check a box" by writing a 90-page "how-to guide" about work stress. It would be an effective way to speak to my clients or help people who don't want to see a counselor. In fact, my original title was going to be *The Work Stress Bill of Rights: 10 Ways to Stop Letting Work Stress Kill You*. Since I have an MBA, a master's in counseling psychology, twenty years in business, and eight years as a therapist, this book was to be a convergence of advice informed by research results from both fields.

However, what I originally wrote came from a shallow and self-centered place. I was giving advice while looking strong and credible. I was preachy and dry and, frankly, I kept sounding like the short articles we've all read when we Google "How to stop a panic attack." The plan was to include a few select portions of the diary I wrote 15 years prior, when I burned out in a country 15,000 miles from home. But it was only to serve as bonus material. I wanted to help the reader engage more and realize they are not the only one going through this private pain.

Then something dawned on me: we don't need more advice. Most of us know what to do to survive a panic attack or decrease work stress.

What we don't know is why we sign up for burnout. We also don't know who we will have to become to surmount it.

So, I've decided to reveal the details of one of the most challenging and dark years of my life. I'm going to show you how I survived it. My story is an intersection of many things: a crisis of faith, being addicted to a job I couldn't do well, fearing I'd lose my husband and son, and wanting to be somebody who mattered. I tell my story through journals, emails, blogs, and online chats. It's a painful, jumbled mashup of my thoughts, but that's exactly how I experienced it. It includes incredible beauty, painful realizations, life-saving love from God, as well as generosity and advice from many others along the way.

It should be noted that I have colleagues at my previous employer who did not share my experience, have had lifelong careers there, and enjoyed their time with the company. Moreover, the decisions and actions I describe in this story occurred many years ago and all employers in this book, and many others worldwide, are making strides to increase awareness and invest in the mental health of their employees.

But, after 15 years of reflection, obtaining my master's in counseling psychology, and the realization that my story might help someone else, I am ready to tell my personal, painful voyage. I'd like to speak compassionately about my burnt-out self and what I could have done differently. I want to tell you where it all started and how I walked away from the things that hurt so badly. I'd like to share how I've come to be emotionally wealthy since that time.

At the end of this book, I share the irrational assumptions and habits that fed my burnout. I have outlined the changes I made, some of them small and surprisingly effective. My hope is that they can help you too.

I'm not going back in time to rescue my younger self. There was a time I wanted so desperately to do that. Instead, I just want to be a good example, or a cautionary tale, whichever you, the reader, need me to be at this moment.

Essentially, this is my way of reminding myself:

You lived through it. It got ugly. You got ugly. But you survived and here's how you did it.

Chapter 1
HOW DID I GET HERE?

February 13, 2006 - Penang, Malaysia

Today I was dropped gently onto the cool, white tiles of reality. Nothing desperate, but nothing beautiful either. Despite the lows I have been expecting, it looks like this week is going to be a good one. I have the right exercise, meals, and activities planned so I can continue my upward climb out of one of the darkest times of my life.

In a few moments, I'll walk with Dave the twenty minutes to Uplands International School to retrieve our seven-year-old son, Sean. We'll walk home on the shady side of a hot street packed with cars and motorbikes. At times, we'll move faster than the traffic. We'll walk alongside the open sewers, not daring to look inside. We'll move past beautiful Buddhist temples, petrol stations, and high-rise apartment buildings.

Back home in our 23rd floor apartment, we'll plot our next adventure, neither of us employed, just sort of catching our breath here in Penang. Someday, when I find the courage and the time, I'll begin to read back over the things I wrote in the journal my best friend gave me as a going away present. I need to answer the question:

"Why did that almost kill me? And how did I get here?"

Tuesday, June 28, 2005

We arrive in Malaysia three days before I am scheduled to begin work this Friday. It's a full 12-hour time difference from Texas. We could not be further from home and jetlag is going to take some time to get over.

We check into a beautiful hotel for a month-long stay in double suites. A large bouquet of flowers greets us.

On Wednesday night, three Nocura directors welcome Dave, Sean and me to Penang with dinner and drinks. Sunday, there is a barbeque planned at the Sales General Manager's apartment overlooking the sea. We will meet lots of expats there. Who could ask for more? Life is good in our new home, even if we're all a little sleepy.

One of the directors, Haruto Ideka, and his wife, Akiko, are the first to officially welcome us to Sean's new school, Penang International, which everyone calls Uplands. I remember Akiko from my 'look-see' visit. She is beautiful and confident and kind—a rare combination. I received an email from her before we even left the US. I feel very fortunate to begin a friendship with Akiko because her husband is the Nocura director I trust most. Haruto is a Nocura veteran who's spent a lot of time marketing in the US. He is in the same division I worked for back in Houston: mobile phones and telephony products. Now I'm marketing components, accessories and consumables in Malaysia, Taiwan, and a few other countries.

Wednesday, June 29, 2005

I've got the worst case of sleep deprivation possible. Jetlag has grabbed hold of my mind. It won't let me shake the cobwebs out of my attic.

We're on the 25th floor of a beautiful high-rise hotel, nestled away in two corner rooms. One has a view of the sea, the other has a view of the city and the hills behind it. The rooms are joined by a central hallway, and a large ornate door allows us to cut off our double suites from the rest of the hotel hall to make one huge private suite.

I am having fun, jumping on the beds (not really), checking out the mini bar, resting a little. But rest is not something I feel comfortable doing. All that's going through my mind is, 'Ohmigosh, what have I talked myself into? They've got me confused with someone else...' But then Pete Gent's football coach from *North Dallas Forty* screams, "Donovan, we hired you because you were smart and fast. Right now, we'd appreciate if you could be just one of those things!" The odd thing is that, because the accommodations are so incredible, I feel even more pressure closing down on my chest.

I pray, 'God, I apologize if I have reached above my capabilities, but could you please help me out here?'

Thursday, June 30, 2005

I prepare everything for an 8:00am arrival at work tomorrow. That's the time my orientation with Haziq, an HR Manager, begins. Even though I know I'll have the first-day-of-school jitters, I want to be ready to go.

The culture of Nocura fits my opinions about work. I've never been called lazy, and I've always tried to be 'Plug and Play' by producing immediately when starting new jobs. I won the 'Top Achiever' award in my US office several times. I have been praised for my level of work and my work ethic. One of the best things my teammates say about me, in any setting, is, "Janna works hard. No one outworks her."

If that's what got me here, what's to stop me from doing it again?

Truth be told, I'm afraid my goals will cause friction between me and Dave. If we argue about work/life balance, I'm sure he'll vote for fewer awards and a little more time at home.

But a can-do attitude is what got me here. I want to be a strong team player, so I've got to stay motivated and find a way to deliver both at work and home.

Friday, July 1, 2005

Three days after arriving, my first day of work at Nocura Asia is here. I iron my long-sleeve power shirt (I'm a director, after all), and I opt for closed toed shoes for my first day. I ask the hotel staff to arrange for a driver for 7:15am, so I can make it to the Nocura facility by 8:00am.

As I climb down into Mr. Gao's car, I swear I can hear a big, padded bar clanging shut, securing me on this amusement park ride. I hear the *chug-chug-chug* of the rollercoaster as it makes its way up the first and tallest set of tracks, gaining maximum momentum for the downhill.

My heart is hammering in my chest. Sweat beads at the

nape of my neck. I have that type of nervous that can only be associated with your first day of work. I love it and hate it at the same time.

We drive toward the international airport, Beyan Lepas Free Trade Zone, and I make it to the office by 8:00am, no small miracle. However, Haziq the HR Manager is nowhere to be found. He shows up a little later with no mention of missing our meeting time. I think to myself, 'Rookie mistake or cultural mistake?'

Gut check number one occurs. I am asked to turn over all three of our passports to a woman who's going to keep them for three days. It is hard to walk away from that woman's desk. I look back longingly at our blue books sitting in a cubbyhole in her cuted-up desk area. Those documents are our only true necessity for international travel. Without them, we have no identity, no country, and no way home... or so it feels on this particular morning.

'I hope she knows what she's doing,' I think as I round the corner to an area of desks and cubicles. This office is full of noisy marketing and engineering teams that support the manufacturing facility.

At my desk, a laptop is waiting for me with everything and anything someone at my level might need. People come by and offer me something to drink and ask if there's anything else they can get me in an oddly deferential way. Why are all these people being so kind to me? That's not the manufacturing culture I was warned about. And why is it so blasted cold in here?

I open my email to find a message from my boss, Juliana, announcing my arrival to the team:

From: Juliana Vásquez, Asia Marketing, CAC
Subject: Janna Donovan, new Director, South Asia Marketing, CAC
This email welcomes Janna Donovan who will direct the marketing efforts for components, accessories and consumables in the Malaysia, Taiwan and Thailand markets. Janna arrives from Nocura US where she managed the marketing of mobile phones and telephony products in the US market. She grew overall revenue 24% YoY. Prior to Nocura, she implemented a system that merchandised and matched 40,000 electronics skus with their consumables for value-added resellers.

Haruto Ideka is the first face I recognize, and he meets me on time at 10:00am. He introduces me to *at least* 30 people over the course of an hour. Walking around with him is like walking around with the mayor of Nocura-town. I do not understand the names. I butcher them immediately. I can't wrap my ears around names like Sheung Hing-Duen and Yau Ching-Lan. I think to myself, 'I've lived in Asia before! It shouldn't be this hard!' But I'm also trying to work through a bad case of jetlag/sleep deprivation. I tell myself it'll be better next week.

Then, gut check number two hits me.

Everyone I meet says they can't wait for me to share my marketing expertise, and that they've been waiting for me for a long time. I think, 'Man, when they find out I'm just one of them, there is going to be some swearing in Mandarin!' Then I say to myself, 'Cool it, Donovan! Take a big, deep breath.' The speed at which emails, peoples' names, and reports flood into my inbox is ridiculously fast. I've got a larger team now so I shouldn't be surprised.

As more emails arrive, I'm buried in a deluge of meeting

requests. At the Daily Product Meeting, we monitor our daily progress toward a quarterly revenue goal in the tens of millions. We display and discuss how each newspaper ad, online banner, and direct mail campaign is meeting its assigned goal for driving sales. I am introduced to another 20 people, half of whom report to me. My first thought is, 'Wow, look at all these people to love.' Weird thought to have in a business meeting, but hey—that's who I am and what I'm ready to do.

As for the business at hand, I don't understand what they're talking about. Not just the Nocura Asia jargon. It's not the English-with-a-different-accent either, because I had learned to be fine with that when Dave and I lived in Tokyo 12 years prior. The issue is with the business metrics and terminologies of my new division. They are completely foreign to me. I've entered what feels like a completely different company, with thinner margins and more pressure.

As morning turns into afternoon, the first email from Dave arrives.

-----Original Message-----
From: David Donovan
To: Donovan, Janna
Subject: How Yew?
I's Fine.
Live simply, expect less, give more.
Dave

-----Original Message-----
From: Janna Donovan
To: David Donovan'

Subject: RE: How Yew?

hi, i'm doing well, have a lot of practice drinking from a fire hose lately, so it's just things as usual. I love you. Big homesick for you and Sean, little homesick for US and texas english and names I can catch right away, but that's to be expected!!!

glad to hear you're fine. I do wring my heart over you and sean and bringing you here. worth the price of admission, worth the price of admission, :o)

At 4:00pm, I have a one-on-one phone call with my boss from her office in Tokyo. Her name is Juliana, and at the end of our call she tells me, "Janna, I want you to come in Monday and be ready to run that Daily Product Meeting."

I think to myself, 'Are you kidding? I'm not qualified to participate in it, let alone run it.'

Then, I pray, 'Oh well, God, can you help with that, too? You created the universe and set it in motion billions of years ago. Surely You can help me learn this little company assignment, right?'

At 5:00pm, Haruto and his driver offer me a ride home, and I gladly take it since I have no cell phone to call a driver or taxi. We head up the winding route through heavy traffic to the northeast part of the beautiful island of Penang, Malaysia, leaving behind the huge Nocura facility.

Dave and Sean aren't in the hotel room when I arrive, so I am very sad, but a little relieved. I slowly lie down on the bed and huddle up into a fetal position as jetlag takes my mind to faraway places.

I survived my first day. Goal met. Target achieved. It is easy to have faith when you're in over your head. *You have no choice.*

It seems oddly easy to stop worrying and let the moments and memories of the day wash over me.

Saturday, July 2 – Sunday, July 3, 2005

I should probably be studying one of the 17 onboarding emails and PowerPoint decks sent from my boss, but I am determined to spend time with Dave and Sean doing something fun, so I'm not doing anything work-related all weekend. I want to practice that work-life balance early and maintain it. I know it's important.

I must walk outside in the sunshine to get over the jetlag, but *uff*, it hurts my brain. I have sleep to catch up on because junkyard dogs guarding the heritage mansion across the street wake me up each night. I must rebuild some energy.

On Sunday, the whole family goes to a huge Pentecostal church. It was exhilarating to see a room full of Asians talking about St. Paul the Apostle and quoting some of my favorite verses, especially one from 2 Timothy 1:

"…the Spirit God gave us does not make us timid, but gives us power, love and self-discipline. … He has saved us and called us to a holy life—not because of anything we have done but because of His own purpose and grace revealed through the appearing of Jesus."

After dinner on Sunday, I look over the onboarding materials, especially the organizational charts. I memorize names and gear up to learn fast. I open my inbox and scan for urgent emails. I take a deep breath and tell myself I am going to build momentum with some small wins this week. I am motivated to succeed, to prove to the powers that be that they were smart to hire me for this opportunity.

Monday, July 4, 2005 – US Independence Day

I'm a little homesick. I wonder what it'll be like living here for two years and whether I can adjust. On the other hand, Dave and I have lived our lives for the stories we can tell, so on I go. The risk-taker mentality in me takes over.

Juliana, my Brazilian boss, arrives in Penang from Tokyo. She is clear and confident and encourages me emotionally and professionally. She provides an incredibly detailed plan for Day One, Week One, Month One, and Quarter One. I am so motivated and think, 'Just keep this deck at hand. All the answers to the test are in here. You might just make it...'

Meetings, meetings, meetings. Metrics, metrics, metrics. At Nocura Asia all events are measured and monitored. It's as cut and dried as one could ever expect. That's why I love whenever I receive emails from Dave.

-----Original Message-----
From: David Donovan
To: Janna Donovan
Subject: Thank you
Janna
I just wanted to say thanks. Thanks for marrying me. Thanks for giving me a son who has become the mirror to improve myself with. Thanks for taking me on the adventure of a lifetime.
I always say with pride that we are not mambee pambee expats, we're going it alone as locals :-), it is a smile every minute. I am so happy. I know things are difficult, but we came here so that things

would be different, at least we can sorta communicate, sometimes, maybe, a little. Mee Goreng next time.
Now to business. I'll talk to Vittoria about Aadya and the car. Not sure I want a car. I love how much I walk. Part of why I'm so happy right now, both physically and mentally. And I think it depends on where we live. I am reminded of the joker's admonition constantly...better be sure.
I love you! Jumpa lagi nanti!!! (see you later, like hasta la vista)
DaveD

After lunch, A VP in Tokyo calls and wants to speak to me on a private line. The VP asks how my first two days have been. As I begin my positive Nocura spin, he interrupts me and says, "I can hear it in your voice that you're coming in low, Janna. You must come in high. I know it takes time to adjust, but you've got to come in high with them when you start."

By this, I think he means, "Janna, you have to hit the ground running. Come in with a high hand or you won't get the chance again!" I feel sick. And mad.

Breathe...unclench your gut, put down the phone. *Click.* I know that I've led people and gotten good results by listening and building trust. It wasn't my style just to hand out orders. I disagree with him, even if it's to my detriment.

As the chaotic day flies by, I email Dave, thinking about Sean.

-----Original Message-----
From: Janna Donovan
To: David Donovan
Subject: RE: A few tings
how was Sean's day?

-----Original Message-----
From: David Donovan
To: Janna Donovan
Subject: RE: A few tings
Sean says 'good'. 'Good because it was fun'. 'Played soccer, i mean football, well soccer is the same thing.' 'Played dodge ball and played stuck in the mud, and crazy asteroids.'

I don't get home from my first Monday until 7:30pm, stuck 40 minutes on the south end of the island without a taxi or a mobile phone. I did not come all this way to never see Dave and Sean!

I finally wave down a taxi and find myself in the back of the cab repeating motivating phrases inspired by my past successes:

"Humility and fierce resolve" – *Good to Great*, Jim Collins.
"Ask for help."

And one I've been saying since my college days: "Don't worry—work."

However, one simple phrase drowns out the others and I use it to laugh within myself: "It seemed like a good idea at the time."

Plus, I am getting lots of encouragement from my family back home. My mom writes:

-----Original Message-----
From: Mom
To: Janna Donovan
Subject: happy 4th
Hi....Janna,
So glad you are making the transition without too much trauma. It

is a difficult task to make your brain realize you have jumped to higher levels and to remind yourself that you are now THE boss...Yea....We all know you have the capabilities to do it so you will rise to the occasion!!!!

Darrel is still in Lubbock...will have the weekend off for the 4th which now dawned on me they do not celebrate the 4th in Malaysia...ha.

Am going to church this am so better run. Love you all sssoooo much!! Thanks for the email.

Love Mom

Tuesday, July 5, 2005

We get an early jump. Anders, a Swede on loan from Nocura Europe, takes several of us "locals" to work every morning at 7:00am because he's hired a driver, Rafeeq, who is very kind and prompt. Juliana, my Tokyo boss, will be here for just a week, so I really want to take advantage of her face-to-face presence. She is positive, direct, clear, and kind. She has picture-perfect command skills, and when you combine it with her Brazilian accent, I'm like a kid with a new favorite teacher.

Sales volume is up, which means that some product or price we advertised is starting to see results. I go to a Daily Review meeting. These people seem so young, yet so good at what they do! I hate the stereotype that comes to my mind: 'Asians are naturally good with math.'

My brain gets exhausted trying to listen to new concepts in Malaysian English that I'm not used to hearing. Are they having difficulty getting used to my Texas English? I need to communicate and understand the team! I don't want others having to repeatedly explain the issues to me.

Sit up straight and *listen*, Janna! I must get different results out of this team if I'm going to survive. Put on your world traveler ears and let's *go*!

Thankfully, the low-grade background stress is subsiding, and I just work on listening to each person as I meet with them. I engage in the moment, and, under no circumstances, do I allow myself to get overwhelmed.

I sit down for lunch with others in the Nocura canteen. Friends in the US would not recognize most of the dishes, except for people who like Indian curries or Thai food.

Our whole team goes out that night to celebrate with Juliana. These people are so friendly and welcoming. I really like them already and they are fun, no doubt about it. I'm happy to be here with them.

I hear some great news about Mark, the VP from the US responsible for most of our results, who first interviewed me for Nocura Asia in Houston. Mark has a reputation as a very hard driver. He's a veteran at Nocura. Make your numbers and you have nothing to worry about. But show weakness or incompetence, and you are D-E-A-D, dead (in Texas, we'd call him a "hard ass"). But it seems he's recently had a personal epiphany about work-life balance and profitability. He is a new man. He's leaving work at a decent hour to see his family and he expects his team to do the same. Miracles never cease.

Juliana says, "Oh, he's done a complete 180. He saw the light when he took a course for VP-level execs. The course is about life balance and using your energy the right way." I tell her I had read about it before coming to Malaysia and I felt motivated just hearing that Mark embraced it.

Life is good. I repeat: *Life. Is. Good.* I smile.

Wednesday, July 6, 2005

Before I arrived in Malaysia, my division took an Employee Survey. So, in my first staff meeting, I present the results to my entire team—definitely comfort-zone central for me.

"Bureaucracy" and "work/life balance" receive the lowest scores. Surprise, surprise. They spend so much time preparing presentations for meetings and then going to meetings, I don't know how they get anything else done.

I must make an inventory of meetings and decks and beg Tokyo for some relief. I understand the execs in Tokyo need frequent information because they are managing us from 5,000 kilometers away, but are the demands for information-gathering and daily presentations getting in the way of us achieving the results they want? Which is more important: making the touchdown or keeping score?

Elizabeth Thompson, the South Asia Sales GM, calls Juliana and me into her office. She asks me what my team's priorities are at this time. I make something up because I'm not sure. She asks if we can add a Back-to-School campaign to our current demand generation efforts. After checking with my team, we decline because of the numerous detailed ad changes it would require and the low demand they think it will generate. I encourage myself, thinking, 'Whew! Way to trust my team and say no in my first week.' It feels good.

I speak with Elizabeth's Administrative Assistant, Janet Huang. I inquisitively look around at all the Christian knickknacks in her cube, and she sees that I'm looking. She says, "You know this is all just chasing after the wind, right? Just take it one day at a time. God knows his purposes. We only see them revealed a little at a time." My eyes widen.

Excellent!

Later that day, an expat from Nocura UK who is ending his assignment in Penang tells me, "Be careful what you ask these people to do. They will say yes and kill themselves trying to do it for you."

As the day rolls along, it seems like my 600-pound guardian angel is working overtime, helping me along my way.

That night, exhausted, I place all my going away cards around the hotel room. They're signed by all my friends back home. Matt's card reminds me to push away the feelings of fear, while Dana and Michele's letters are full of encouragement. I can even tell members of GreatHopeGals, my church small group back home, are praying for me. But what happens if they stop? I'm cooked.

All week, emails and prayers have come in from everyone. I receive a wonderful note from my mom, and I respond to her with a little more sunshine than I really feel. I have to loosen up.

I need to get the Tokyo VP's comment about "coming in high" out of my head. I tell myself, 'Maybe you are over-reacting. No one around here is looking for you to fail.'

Thursday, July 7, 2005

I give performance reviews to two people on my team, with Juliana taking the lead. Our most important manager, Luke, has had two resignations under him recently and we're a little concerned about that. His team manages all advertising placements in every South Asia market. Essentially, they keep the phones ringing and the whole engine running.

As a routine part of the review, Juliana asks him to estimate his risk of leaving. Luke tells her his risk of leaving is actually "high." He wants something more out of his life than working all day and night.

My heart begins to pound as I think to myself a little prayer, 'God, help me. Is Juliana listening to what this guy is saying?' She appears optimistic and nonplussed. But this is my fourth official day at work, and this is not news that I can hear and remain cool and neutral. We are already down 10 on a team that is supposed to number 25. Luke is *the* key manager on my team, and I cannot afford to lose him.

I think, 'God, you've asked me not to worry. It's hard to comply! I don't know how to do what Luke does. I don't want to sleep here on a little cot!'

I decide to unplug instead of stressing, and I celebrate this fine Thursday by going home at 5:15pm. I sit down for dinner with Sean and Dave, and I'm just so happy to see them and relax. They are my lifeline.

Friday, July 8, 2005

I'm tired, but not too cranky. The driver comes at 7:00am. I'm ready because I skip the hotel buffet and have a hard-boiled egg at the Nocura canteen instead. I start another day of back-to-back-to-back meetings.

There's something that's really bugging me. My whole team is in each and every meeting I attend. I want to say, "Shouldn't you be out there working on all the stuff we gave you to do at this morning's meeting? We're wasting your time!"

But I don't.

During the second meeting of the day, I solicit ideas for banner ads that will successfully promote peripherals, and a Nocura veteran says, "Yes, we did it in India and the US." I agree and tell her I think it'll work here. She says, "I'll get the team together and we'll be back at your cube for 10:30."

Six people, including a Brand Manager, show up at 10:30am, ready to turn big dollar ads around on a dime. I remember the word of caution I was given just days earlier: "They will say yes and kill themselves trying to do it for you." It's already happening, and a stab of guilt runs through me.

Somehow, I squeeze in two more meetings before noon, then I decide to buy my immediate team lunch because, hey, it's Friday, and they've been working their asses off all week. For the five of us it costs 26 Malaysian Ringitt or $6 US. I try to be all "local" and eat stuff I don't like much, but my whole team lines up at the fish-n-chips station—by far the most popular service line. Why am I such a try-hard?

I have yet another after-lunch meeting and then follow it up with the dreaded last meeting of the day, where the goal is to solicit the vendor for funding in home and small business sales. Word around the office is that vendor representatives have been so rude to my team in the past that a Nocura exec had to stop the meeting and ask them to be more professional.

Partners from larger cities seem to look down on us in Penang because we are often treated as the backwater, second city of Malaysia. Maybe it's true that we're the younger brother from the village, but I also know that vendors just try to intimidate us.

The meeting starts, and I think, 'This is it. They're gonna find out what a novice I really am.' The vendor once again demands sales data that Nocura has refused to give them. I stick to my guns on what performance data we'll provide, and no one bats an eye. We then accept many of their ideas and, to everyone's surprise, the meeting ends on a really positive note with everyone smiling and glad they came. They give us more than our fair share of Asia's dollars for our proposed programs. And they give me a personal gift valued just low enough to be legit, so I accept it. It's a copy of a popular video game for my seven-year-old son.

'God, now you're just showing off!' I flippantly pray. 'I mean, a hotel by the sea, relationships that have bonded quickly, saying no and protecting my people in the first week. That I can understand. But to have a meeting with *that* vendor go well? C'mon! You have seriously outdone Yourself.'

In the taxi on the way home, Juliana's voice sounds great on my new company mobile phone, "You're already contributing, Janna. Well done." More inspiration comes into my head from pithy bumper stickers and motivational books. "Today's great oak is just yesterday's nut that held its ground."

I think, 'Absolutely unbelievable. Hallelujah!' I sound like one of those football players on TV who thanks Jesus after he wins. What about the people on the other team? Doesn't God wish them equally as much happiness and success? Oh well, I can't think about that right now. I am too busy doing the happy dance!

I feel like I'm riding a bicycle on a high-wire. So, look at me quickly while I'm still balancing, world! Because I have to go back to work next Monday and try to do it again!

But so far, things, while stressful, are going really well, because I'm diving in headfirst and figuring it out as I go. This isn't the first time either.

It was the same at my previous job working for a dot-com. I would beg, borrow, and steal resources from all over the company to get stuff done. But, looking back, I was one part martyr and one part wannabe hero. I took a thirty percent cut in pay and worked thirty percent more hours. The CEO and CIO took whatever I was willing to give, which was everything.

For a while, no one noticed my efforts at the dot-com. I thought no one was grateful for the amount of energy and worry I put into my work, so I had to be satisfied with my own successes.

When the company president finally noticed, he said, "We couldn't have done this without you," and he rewarded me with better projects and a raise. I didn't care if co-workers blamed my leaders for playing favorites when they promoted me. Annoying as it sounds, I thought I deserved it!

Not only did I work, but I also worried. I did enough worrying for the entire company. Throughout my life, when I didn't worry that's when everything went wrong. I told myself that I was doing everyone a favor when I stressed *more* at work. So stress I gladly did!

At the dot-com, I was fixated on details and addicted to emptying my inbox. I think my boss, the CEO, and even the Board saw my obsessive tendencies and work stress as a good thing, because when they asked for results, they knew they could trust me to figure out the *how*. It was a hard-charging, take-no-prisoners culture, and I thought I had solved the best way to survive and thrive.

When I left the dot-com, I took that "hero mentality" to Nocura US. I was only there for a few weeks when my teammates warned me, "It's a shame, Janna. We like you, but we are going to miss you."

"What? I'm a star!" I replied, grinning.

They told me, "You should pace yourself. If you keep going at this pace you will be used up and spit out."

That hasn't happened yet. And it won't happen here either.

When 7:00pm on Friday night rolls around, the fun doesn't stop. Dave, Sean, and I still don't have a home, so we look at a beautiful, furnished apartment with a gorgeous pool. Then, we interview a "maid." I hate that label, for a lot of reasons. Anyway, she actually interviews us, and we love her. We are hired. Her name is Aadya.

As we start home, I discover that Sean has a swollen lymph gland under his arm. Could it be caused by the Hepatitis A or typhoid shot he had prior to coming? Has he gotten one of the conditions we were warned about, including encephalitis? We were told to get vaccinated for it once we arrived, but we haven't had the time. Or we haven't *taken* the time.

We go to a premier hospital in Penang that's two doors down from our hotel. An extremely polite, efficient receptionist helps us. We see the doctor after just 15 minutes. He's been educated in Malaysia, Scotland, and the UK and specializes in pediatric cardiology. He is so kind to Sean, I'm amazed. He prescribes antibiotics and then *walks us down the hall to the hospital pharmacy* that's still open at 8:30pm on a Friday. With medication in our hands, we are home by 9:00pm.

My respect for Malaysia and the island of Penang has just doubled and tripled tonight. The humility and confidence and warmth of the people are amazing. And to have a doctor act in such a kind manner? It's only added to an absolutely powerful start to our Malaysian experience. This first week has been an incredible rollercoaster ride.

Next week? To freaking Thailand to ride some elephants! So excited! The blessings don't stop. I don't really deserve any of it. Yes, I work hard, but I've done a lot of things in my life that weren't right and hurt the ones I love. But God gives forgiveness, and He is changing me. Time to go forward in life and let good things happen. Thank you, Lord Jesus. Praise God from whom all good things flow.

Chapter 2
DON'T WANNABE A WANNABE

Sunday, July 9, 2005 – Penang, Malaysia

I keep thinking about the long journey I took to get here. How did I even get the nerve to take this risk, to go on this life-changing adventure? What is it in my makeup or background that brought me to this place, to this moment? I think back to 2004.

I wasn't actually chosen by the true powers at Nocura. I was a mid-level marketing person who set unit-shipment records for mobile phones. To find success, I used my experience as an IT business analyst and marketer.

Then, one day, Nocura HR sent out an email asking for people interested in working in Asia, so I raised my hand and expressed interest. Furthermore, Dave thought it would be an adventure he could sign up for. He encouraged me to check things out, and I began the long interview process.

I'm not the type of employee Nocura normally sends abroad. Most candidates for expatriate positions are chosen by management to develop their long-term potential for success at higher levels within the company. But I figured I could fight for what I wanted just like the high potential types. I thought I'd swing for the fences. The desire to make it "over there" has been alive in me since I was a small child.

I was used to going around obstacles my entire life. I went to college at 17, graduated at 20 with good grades, and managed to make it into a top 20 MBA program at the University of Texas where, to everyone's surprise, I won the Outstanding Student Award when I graduated. Raising my hand for an overseas assignment was no different. I knew I could do it if they gave me the chance to prove myself. I'd won the lottery in the world of work many times.

In my late twenties, after completing an executive training program as a retail buyer, I married Dave and he started working for a family-owned business. After working as a financial analyst and then assistant buyer, I wanted to strike out on my own. I went to apply for a stock-girl position at my retailer's outlet store, so I could be underemployed while I decided what kind of business to start. However, even though I arrived dressed for a stock-girl interview, they offered me the store manager position.

I agreed before I knew the store was losing money every year and their plan was to shut it down and lay off the employees. Two months into working there, I called the CFO and asked him, "If this store makes money, will you keep it open?"

He laughed and said, "Yes."

We turned it around by going back to what made the

"real" stores work. We made the store look less like an outlet store and more like a place where you could find designers at deep discounts. We showed the designer lines as they were supposed to be shown. We solidified our relationships with fashionista customers, and we decreased how much merchandise value we were losing because of confusion, theft, and poor inventory practices. When we started to turn a big profit, the company followed suit and opened a bunch more outlet stores loosely based on what they'd learned from our success.

I did not think of myself as a hero back then. I just wanted to see how high I could go. No matter the job, I found myself accepting extra work when it was piled on even when my managers didn't provide me with the staff I was budgeted for. How could I argue or complain? I didn't want to lose the respect and admiration of my bosses.

What I did not realize was that it was becoming a habit.

I became the "go to" person. It's just what I did, at home and at work. I wouldn't let people down, hurt their feelings, or make them mad. I couldn't say "wait!" or "no" because I felt too much guilt. I distrusted those who said, "Stop working on what doesn't matter", "Prioritize," or "Focus" because I thought they were trying to take away my strength! If you had a problem, I would try to solve it. Being needed was a call I had to answer.

Above all, I wanted a reputation as a hard worker. I saw that the "Subject Matter Expert" (SME) title came with plenty of job security and chances at leadership. So, I volunteered for a high workload. It felt great to be engaged, and it fueled camaraderie because my teammates respected me. I got what I wanted: praise, recognition, meaning, and connection.

Work made me feel strong, legitimate, and trustworthy. I cared a great deal about my work. I thought of it as my way of helping others. I might not have been saving lives as a first responder or teaching underserved children, but I felt that anything I did to move the team ball forward would help others' lives, and in many cases, I was right. People would contact me several years later to tell me what a positive effect my leadership had on their lives and dreams.

I guess I was comfortable in the hero role, and that spilled into my work at Nocura.

But, after eight months of emails back and forth and several interviews for the overseas position, I wasn't feeling much like a hero. I finally told Nocura I was not interested in moving from Houston, Texas if it involved a cut in pay. What Nocura Malaysia proposed was unreasonable given the increased cost of expat living in Penang. So, I wrote one last email asking what kind of experience Nocura Asia would consider valuable. What would they pay a reasonable amount for in the future? My new plan was to move within Nocura US to one of the highly valued areas and then interview again in two years for a position in Southeast Asia.

I began looking for that new spot in Nocura US, and I kept working long hours. I joked with a colleague, "What I ought to do is resign and become a 'Rest Consultant' for everyone around here. If there's no such thing, I'll make one up."

But then my plans changed again. Nocura Malaysia contacted me and said they wanted me to interview for a Director position, which would give them more room to compete with my US salary. The decision-maker for that position would be back in the US for just two weeks and agreed to do an initial interview with me.

The VP who interviewed me, Mark Denning, was someone I liked from the moment I met him. I wanted to please him. I was confident and I talked about how important it was to me to be a good manager. He must have liked what he heard, because four new interviews were scheduled immediately for the next week; a week I was planning on taking off for spring vacation.

I had two of the interviews by phone while at work in Houston. The first was with two directors in Nocura Asia Marketing and the other was with the Sales General Manager, Elizabeth Thompson, who was one of the bosses to whom I would be reporting. Colleagues from every continent. What a happy xenophile I was!

After I got the green light from these three people, I drove to New Mexico to see my parents and get Sean, who was staying with them for Spring Break. The sun shone brightly and hot as I drove the long trip alone, leaving the plains of Texas and climbing the mountains to their place. It was an incredible day for a drive, sunny and clear.

In the car, I practiced for the most important interview of my life. It was with the VP who looked over the area Nocura called "South Asia." To prepare, I phoned friends who had experience with these countries—especially India, because I reasoned that the largest country in that zone would be the focus of the interview.

When I arrived at my parents', I stretched my legs and had some of my mother's time-tested comfort food: pinto beans and Texas corn bread (no sugar, lots of bacon grease). The following morning, we awoke to a deep carpet of snow over the golf course behind my parents' house. It stretched over the mountains, trees, and cars. Sean and I bundled up and went outside to make mounds of giant snowballs so we could build a snow bridge across the creek. After a few snowball fights, we went up to the clubhouse where we jumped into the steaming hot swimming pool and swam and played for a while. All of this was meant to relax my nerves before the big interview that afternoon, but it was only slightly effective.

Breaking the silence, my mom's voice came searing across the silent, deserted golf course. "Janna, there's someone on the phone from Nocura."

'Oh no,' I thought. 'I've got the wrong time for the interview and now I'll be all winded and unprepared…' With a clinched stomach and tense jaw, I took the phone and realized that it was a good friend from Nocura US who'd chased me down. He understood that I wanted the scoop on Nocura India and, being from there, he wanted to help me out. I welcomed it, but the false alarm left me tense for the call.

6:00pm finally came. Family members went out to dinner so I could concentrate on the VP interview with no noise or distractions. I had read about Jakob DeVries on the internet. I knew where he'd worked before, his accomplishments, and the prestigious schools he'd attended.

When the conversation began, I could hardly talk I was so nervous. The weight of what I knew about him hurt instead of helped in this situation. He was jovial and positive. I was stiff as a board, not my outgoing self, even screwing up the exchange of pleasantries at the start and finish of the interview. I secretly prayed that my few words would be construed as a serious, no-nonsense demeanor, because that was what I was supposed to be like, right?

He asked about my experience with the dot-com selling IT products, so I shared with him how we grew from zero to

40 million in annual sales. I described how I'd helped lead a strategy overhaul, in which we went from selling to individual customers to selling to small businesses. This was something I knew he'd find relevant. Then I explained how I'd achieved my numbers at Nocura in recent quarters, giving Nocura's distribution network a fast and accurate way to order telephones.

He asked how I enjoyed Japan in 1993. I told him I loved the people, but I didn't work for Nocura in Japan. Instead, I was an expat wife who supported her husband by joining him in Tokyo when he worked there. I did not tell him that Dave's "expatriate preparation" consisted of a senior VP seeing him in the gent's room and asking him if he liked sushi. We still laugh about that.

The VP also asked what my family thought of moving to Malaysia. I loved to answer this question because I was so keen to give my son, Sean, an international experience, to help him see things from more than just an American point of view. Even better, Dave and Sean were excited to go. I told him about Dave and I's 1996 trip through Malaysia and that we were looking forward to the weather. Summer year-round!

The interview ended, my parents and son returned, and I told them I'd done the best I could. I was happy either way the decision went.

What a horrible liar I was.

The HR interview happened the next night while I was still on vacation. When the Nocura Malaysia HR executive, Stephen Davis, came on the line, he hinted that I had made it past the interviews, so I was free to celebrate with my family. His final words of advice to me were, "Make developing your people your priority. Even if you don't make your numbers, develop your people."

'Pffft,' I thought. 'I'll do both!'

In business, you develop an understanding that you must do whatever it takes to ethically make your numbers. Period. You have to develop your people to make your numbers.

They asked me to fly over for a site visit, but when it came time to pay for the flight, the funds from Nocura didn't make it to me in time, so I bought the ticket myself. Undaunted, I said goodbye to Dave and Sean and boarded the flight for Dallas, then flew to Hong Kong and on to Penang.

I was driven from the airport to the Equatorial Hotel. I thought I'd be fine with the heat, but the air was thick. As I entered the elevator to go freshen up in my room, the heat felt heavy on my chest and made it hard to breathe. It was like being trapped in a sauna.

When the HR host picked me up at the hotel, he caught me off guard by asking, "You're married aren't you, Janna? Where is your husband?"

How embarrassing! How weird! I did not know that Dave was included in the invitation.

The site visit went well. I was enthusiastic and tried not to let jetlag produce any stupid answers. It wasn't hard, however, because almost as soon as I landed, I was back on a plane so I could be in Houston for work on Monday. The trip was quick, and the site visit was just a taste.

When I arrived home, there was one more hurdle to overcome: salary negotiations. The offer for the director position came in at 85% of my US salary, which I was fine with. But there was a twist. I wouldn't be reporting to the

Sales GM in Penang. I'd report to a Marketing Director based in Tokyo.

After all the time we'd spent mulling over everything, Dave was not the picture of enthusiasm. He reminded me that I was agreeing to work in a division of the company I'd never worked in before. He had read that different divisions were like different companies within Nocura. Moreover, the cost-of-living issue was still a problem, and now he was whispering loudly in my ear, "Remember, they know the slew of problems you're walking into! You don't!"

So, taking Dave's advice, I declined the offer for the second time and tried not to think of the eight months of my life I had just invested in my expat dream.

But they wouldn't let it go in Asia. The following night, the headhunter from Tokyo called once more to see how the gap could be closed. Dave couldn't understand why I was even on the phone. We'd said no and we were getting on with our lives, right? Right?!

Before I hung up the phone, she'd doubled the signing bonus and provided me another concession, making it a little over 90% of my US salary. I let her know we'd think about it.

Dave stormed out the front door screaming something unrecognizable. He was furious. By the time he came back in, I was screaming too. "I want to do this! All we've ever been are wannabes! We say we're going to live out our dreams, do incredible things, then we don't do them! I'm tired of it. This is my chance to become something more than a wannabe."

I can't remember if I definitively stated, "We are going!" but that was the general message Dave received. After we calmed down, Dave opened the spreadsheet, added the additional signing bonus to our calculations and said, "Say yes if you want to. Just make a decision one way or the other. I want to get on with my life."

What followed was ten weeks of packing, partying, and sending FedEx documents overseas. Official copies of college and grad school diplomas had to be provided, and I had a hard time understanding which thing Nocura was demanding and which the Malaysian government required.

As I went through the motions, I had a constant weight of feeling underprepared. I had not previously worked in the CAC division, nor had I held a director-level job at Nocura. So, I initiated an informal mentorship program while I waited to move. I talked with many people across Nocura who knew the job I was about to do. Even with their packed schedules, all these directors and managers were willing to share their precious time and advice with me.

I had a series of telephone one-on-ones with my new boss, Juliana. I liked her instantly. Like Dave, her husband had also retired from the corporate world to manage his investments. She had a young son that she adored. She talked a lot about being a manager who developed people and told me I'd find out more about that when I arrived.

Dana and JB, our great friends, threw us a huge Texas barbeque as a Going Away Party. Tents were set up at our house in Houston and there were horseshoe competitions with our televisions as prizes (they wouldn't work in Malaysia). It was an incredible time to see and hug all the people we loved, and I took every opportunity to let them know it in mushy notes or heart-to-heart talks.

Everyone commented on the love they felt under the tents and among the hay bales that Saturday night. I could still feel that emotion and community the next morning when everyone had gone. I sat under the pecan tree and watched Sean wrestle the party supplier's portable bar to the street to sell lemonade, complete with a blue gingham tablecloth and a homemade sign.

That night, Mike and Madeline, our neighbors and close friends, took us to dinner and then to the airport hotel. I was emotionally exhausted from saying goodbye to so many people. We boarded the flight then had an extended layover in Tokyo so we could take a rest and eat at some restaurants that were favorites back when we lived there in 1993. Finally, with excitement and a sense of risk, Dave, Sean and I went on to Penang.

Now that we're here, it feels almost surreal—like I don't belong. Will I ever get used to this? What about Sean?

Only time will tell. I have to put everything I have into making this work. For us, and for everyone that believes in me.

Chapter 3
A BABY ELEPHANT AND THE DECISION TO FIGHT

Saturday, July 16, 2005 - Penang, Malaysia to Ch'iang Mai, Thailand

We've only been here for two weeks and, before we know it, I have a three-day weekend. So, we find ourselves on our way to Ch'iang Mai, Thailand with my Sales GM, Liz, as well as her friends visiting from Australia.

We get up Saturday for a very early flight, touch down in Ch'iang Mai and check into the hotel at around 11:00am. We have lunch and head for the pool to play games with our three boys, all the same age. As I lay back on the lounge chair with a fruity drink, I say, "This is the first time I've truly relaxed in ten months," to no one in particular. We go out for Thai food but end up eating Penang Chicken (which we've never had in Penang) and order burgers for the kids.

The next day, Sunday, we put on our trekking gear with great anticipation. We are going to spend the day up close and personal with elephants. We arrive in the countryside where the elephants are penned in a large enclosure that looks like a Wild West horse pen for giants. With them looking over the huge railings at us, it is like seeing a llama in a farm petting zoo, only much larger and smellier.

We watch the mahouts bathe the elephants in the river. As we get closer to watch, one of the bigger elephants dips its trunk in the water and covers us in river water. It is magical and quite fun, touristy stuff, and exactly what we all needed.

The mahouts put our boys, one by one, on the biggest and smartest elephant so we can take their photos. Then, each elephant is fitted with a special blanket and box to enable two tourists to ride on its back.

Eventually, Sean and I hop on, then the elephants wade through the water and begin our trek through the jungle. It honestly looks a little like central Texas to me, not too exotic. But Thai jungle it is, so we are going to enjoy it.

We pass "viewing stands" with thatched roofs, built tall enough for us to pay for, reach out, and take packages of elephant food. It feels like we are expected to buy the food, so we do. No matter—it's fun watching the elephants eat.

Each elephant box is equipped with a sun-reflecting silver umbrella, so we hoist ours to escape some of the searing rays that are beating down. We are enjoying it, but without the umbrella we'd be like a sausage in a convenience store, left to bake on the hot rollers with no way to get out. Finally, we come to a small village where the people don't seem very Thai or even authentically dressed, but they certainly are enthusiastic to show us their items for sale. The elephants lumber up to another large viewing stand built against a steep hillside and let us disembark. Sean and I head straight for the cool drinks. Fanta and Sprite are ubiquitous worldwide, thank goodness. The other mothers and kids head toward the little market to shop.

Sean and I race to catch up with the others already buying trinkets. As we move down the short, steep hill, we run into a baby elephant giving himself a dirt bath by taking the loose dirt on the hillside with his trunk and spraying it all over his back. 'Good for the skin!' I think. 'How cute!'

With Sean beside me, we pet him on his forehead, and then, BAM! The little elephant plunges right into Sean with that same forehead, knocking him back against the steep hill. Sean is pinned against the hill and slides down to the baby elephant's feet. I scream and push on the baby as hard as I can, but he keeps slowly moving forward. All I can focus on is the dinner-plate-sized foot hovering above Sean's knee, poised to come down on it.

I intently watch to see if the elephant will put it down and stand on Sean's leg. I keep expecting that super-human-mother strength you hear about to kick in—you know, the kind that helps a tiny woman lift a taxi off a pedestrian—but I don't feel it. I just keep leaning on the elephant and yelling like you'd yell at a bully, "Get OFF of him! Get OFF of him! Get OFF!"

In a flurry, three mahouts surround us and begin to beat the little elephant with the non-sharp end of their mahout stick, created for just such occasions as this. The little elephant runs to his mother's side, and she walks off deliberately with him trailing her. To me, she seems to say, "I told you not to do stuff like that. You know I can't do anything if the people with the sticks get mad." It is over in two minutes.

I am jarred back to reality by the sound of Sean screaming. I check him all over, then stand him up. We climb back up the little hill to the drink stand and sit in the shade. All the staff surround us, and the kids and parents come running. They try to make Sean feel better by saying this is how baby elephants show they want to play, that Sean is lucky to have been chosen. They also say that Orange Fanta is the little elephant's favorite drink and he wanted Sean to share.

The only blood spilled is from my knee, which is bleeding from kneeling on the hill as I pushed against the 800-pound elephant. I am trying to laugh to help Sean forget about it, but my body is shaking uncontrollably and I can't slow my breath.

For two straight nights, lightning strikes within my deepest sleep and I awake startled and shaking several times. Not to rainstorms, but to the scene of that little elephant butting Sean with his head and pushing him down, ready to fight or play. I just have difficulty forgetting.

We return from Thailand to Penang late Monday night, around 11:00pm. Dave and I would never have scheduled a return that allowed so little recovery time before work the next day, but, oh well, what the heck? We are on the adventure of our lives. Not wannabes any longer, *are* we! Woo-hoo!

Tuesday, July 19, 2005

The next day, I am back at work for a short week. I attend some of my first meetings with the VPs. They are long meetings with ten of us on a conference room speakerphone speaking with Mark Denning, while he is traveling to markets larger than ours in India and Australia.

A Finance VP asks us to explain how we will increase prices to achieve the margin plan in the upcoming quarter. *It is my sixth day in this job.* I have no idea how they price accessories/components or how the margin plans fit together. I don't even know the offerings that well because I worked with phones back in the US. This is all new to me.

I sit and think of this analogy: I've been training in the paratrooper division back home... "Rangers lead the way!" But when I get to the battlefield, I am asked to be a tank commander with a totally different kind of team using completely different skills and knowledge.

I think, 'Maybe this switch wasn't such a good idea? Or am I whining unnecessarily?' Maybe some of both.

I wonder if the cold conference room is causing me to shake uncontrollably or whether it might have something to do with the pressure I'm feeling. Again, maybe some of both. I try to hide it and the shaking finally subsides. Is that what a panic attack feels like?

The meeting continues for three hours. I don't remember ever having a three-hour meeting in the US except once a quarter for a performance review. It seems execs, especially at Nocura, want you to state your performance, explain your plan, be brief, and leave. Or perhaps because I wasn't a director in the US, maybe I wasn't needed in the meetings for all three hours?

I go through the rest of the week tired and stressed, feeling uninformed and incompetent. As the week goes along, I keep getting told that, "Isaiah is going to join your team. He'll be transferred in this week, but you can't have his temp. You good with that?"

"Great!" I say. "Many hands make light work even without the temp! Good for us!"

What I naively forgot to ask is, "Does Isaiah bring any quota with him?"

Of course he does! His additional area almost doubles the sales I am responsible for generating. I get *one* guy and my quota is doubled?

That high-wire bicycle I was on? Yeah, it's already hit the street below and I'm hanging onto the wire by my fingertips. But, no matter what, I have to get back on the wire. That's just the way it goes.

Then, I am given another project on top of all the country projects I already have going. The company tells me it's imperative that all of South Asia's operations in Penang have standard operating procedures that protect the privacy of our customers' sensitive information. It becomes my job to manage a process for all other directors and their teams ensuring all rules are in place and executed. To me, and any other sane person, this seems like a full-time job in and of itself.

But hey...that's the way it goes.

I catch a ride home Friday afternoon with Liz and some others, mostly Europeans. The head of Marketing in another product division, Ian Taylor, rides with us. He asks how Ch'iang Mai was and I ignore all the moments of relaxation, fun, and good food, and say, "To be honest, Ian, a little elephant stole some of my magic." After I tell him the story of Sean and the elephant, I immediately regret it.

All this week, after I've shared the story, no one else has seen the fear and danger in it. Maybe it's cultural? Maybe Americans get more worked up about safety than other people? Maybe we're just big babies compared to Asians and Europeans?

In the US, we build railings around the Grand Canyon to protect people from themselves. By contrast, other countries seem to say, "Visitor beware: don't be stupid and you won't get hurt." I have always admired that as a world traveler, scuba diver, and backpacker. I guess an 800-pound elephant will take some of the smart alec out of you. I hate being negative with colleagues, but I can't help myself. I'm tired.

It takes a lot of faith and trust to parent in a country not your own. This morning, Dave felt he had no choice but to let Sean ride alone in a taxi in order to get him to school on time.

-----Original Message-----
From: David Donovan
To: Janna Donovan
Subject: What a day

Janna, so strange to put sean into a taxi by himself. by the time the taxi arrived the rain had passed and i felt like i should walk with him. we could have walked anyway, but today seemed like as good a day as any to let him go. i'm very sad though. he is growing up and out of our hands very fast. next time ask for more vacation.
the limo lady called a "special" taxi...i guess someone she was familiar with to let sean ride with someone she knew instead of just the next guy in line. made me feel good, and she was very sweet. i'm a little worried sean will leave his backpack in the taxi and not have his stuff for the field trip, and worse be kicking himself for being stupid all day. i love and need you. we all need each other so much during these days of transition. please take care of yourself, block your calendar for 30 mins and go eat lunch, or just find a quiet

place (at Nocura, funny) and sit and relax. you must take care of yourself.
Jumpa lagi nanti
DaveD

Saturday, July 23, 2005

I feel alone and vulnerable. There seems to be no one I can trust with my secret self-doubt and exhaustion. I must think of others. Other people are working in tougher conditions with fewer resources and more at stake. I have a point to prove. *Get up.* Do something different.

I've heard about Penang International Church. I've searched for it and asked all around but cannot find it. So, we continue to go to the Pentecostal church. A friendly woman named Joyce takes us home from the service in the rain. She works at Sean's school, and when she comes into the hotel lobby with us, she bumps into another teacher named Sylvia Rajamoney. Sylvia turns out to be Sean's teacher at Uplands. She has just walked out of a service for the Penang International Church. It meets in the very hotel where we are staying! Biggest, loveliest coincidence and a smile for the day.

At a barbeque later that day in the VP's high-rise apartment, a master's student and I strike up a conversation that sticks with me. He says, "You know, a common theme among executives is that they're afraid someone will find them out and realize they're not nearly as smart or talented as everyone wishes they were. It's called the Imposter Syndrome."

My mouth nearly drops to the floor. Surely he is not aware of my private struggle! Well, if I didn't think it was real, now

I do, because there's a name for it.

Monday, July 25, 2005

On the way out the door, I grab Dave's blue fleece jacket, the only coat any of us brought to Malaysia. I'm tired of shivering and I've lost a little weight, so it's huge on me.

I go to work with the thought of doing something for others and to stop obsessing about my own problems. I write an email to the top-ranking human resources exec who first interviewed me. He seems able to connect Dave and me with a charity that helps children in Cambodia.

-----Original Message-----
From: Stephen Davis
To: Janna Donovan
Subject: RE: Helping in Cambodia
Janna,
The best way is for me to get you in touch with my wife.
We fell in love with Cambodia over 2 years ago and helped start this charity. Naturally we have been very passionate about it. We just got back in May and took over 75 people (mostly high school youth group) for 5 days to build homes and work on the school. It is a truly amazing place.
However, I would strongly suggest that the first thing you need to do is try and go visit. My wife can get you in contact with the right hotels, guides, etc. You should go visit the school, meet the children, see the amazing temples and look at all we are doing. From there you can decide what you want to do.
Let me know if you have any questions. Thanks, Stephen

I research the charity, and, for a brief time, I feel calmer. I think of someone else and how hard they have fought for survival. That briefly takes my mind off myself and makes me feel like less of a whiner.

Taking action, though, is what will make me feel like my old self. But I have no idea when we can go and visit the school. Dave says he's open to traveling to Siem Reap in northwestern Cambodia where a huge religious structure sits. People go there to see the ruins of Angkor, where the Khmer Kingdom was ruled from the 9th–15th centuries.

I make it a priority to plan a trip there, and possibly elsewhere in Cambodia. I need something to look forward to, an escape from work where I can redirect my focus to those in need.

I need to feel useful again.

Chapter 4
IT'S TIME TO DO SOMETHING

Tuesday, July 26, 2005 - Penang, Malaysia

The quarter is about to end. Sales are looking good, but my profit margin is not. The upcoming quarter is looming large, and numbers must be made. Moreover, employee survey scores have tanked in crucial areas and improvements must begin now.

Desperate times call for desperate measures, so I decide to bear down and work even harder. Get on the treadmill and run till I can't run any longer.

I come from a long line of people who know how to work hard. I am truly and always inspired by my grandmothers, each of whom survived two world wars and the Great Depression, obtained their college education, raised four children in western Texas, and sent a son to Vietnam.

If I'm not pedaling the bicycle fast enough, I need to pedal faster. I just can't take time off anymore if what I'm doing is not enough. I'm usually alert, energetic, and wired. Being wired helps me keep grinding. All this is an adrenaline rush. But right now, it's becoming very difficult to break out of the gravitational pull of work, to even think about taking a week off, going to Cambodia, or doing something besides work.

Even when I do schedule time off, my mind does not cooperate. It does not know I am supposed to be resting. When I schedule a massage, I can't enjoy the massage because my mind is not relaxed. If I'm thinking about work and trying to solve work problems while I'm home, I might as well be at work!

My day starts at 5:00am with the Buddhists chanting and burning incense across the main street. I jog around my apartment tower's beautiful grounds—about a city block. I take time to reflect and eat breakfast. Then, when I hear the 6:00am Muslim call to prayer, it is time to jump in the shower. At 6:30am, Rafeeq, who has now become my regular driver, arrives downstairs in the circular drive of my high-rise. I arrive at the office at 7:00am.

I work on the 100 new emails waiting for me and prepare for a week of back-to-back meetings. I plan to do a better job of monitoring sales hourly, especially since the info is tracked every two hours and then compared to a detailed, hourly forecast. If our ads don't result in someone in Malaysia, Singapore, Thailand or Taiwan ordering consumables or PC accessories, we have to know why. It is that simple. What's wrong with the price, the weekly special, or manufacturer co-marketing? I resolve to set my team's recovery tactics into motion much sooner in the day if recovery is what's needed.

When I spoke with Human Resources during my site visit, I got the sense that I would be dealing mostly with Malays. I always think back to my 1996 visit to Malaysia and remember Malaysians as gentle, fun-loving, sometimes quiet people. I was mentally prepared to not act like the overbearing, loud-mouth, bossy, direct, and selfish Texan before I arrived. You know... *me*. But I am so far off in my projections of what is needed of me in this workplace!

The Chinese ethnicity dominates the areas of Nocura that I work in, and I've formed the opinion that no "development" of them is needed as had been suggested. I try to resist stereotypes but am continuously struck by what strong businesspeople my Chinese colleagues are. I hate to use the word "hardened," but they know their stuff. They are never caught unprepared. In status meetings, they rattle off their numbers like someone reading a weathercast. "Quick check on Taiwan shows daily demand is at 92% and conversion is at 104% of goal."

No matter what the executives ask of them, they stay late and finish it. They rarely go to lunch outside the building, and they sit through long meetings without complaint. They are just *hard*, and even when they fight with one another to get something done, they go out arm in arm to implement their decisions. I feel like a reluctant slave driver with a willing and bonded team of miners.

My executives advise me to ask people to leave meetings if they show up unprepared. Am I missing something? Who is unprepared? And even if someone is unprepared, when the hell are they supposed to prepare? They are *always* in meetings. If they are unprepared, I just don't see it!

However, a thought won't leave me alone when I hear the execs ask us to show more initiative—something I was taught early in my career. If you take away the respect for a person's decisions, their autonomy, soon they will not be able to make decisions even if you ask them to.

Am I overreacting? As the egalitarian, blue-collar American who was taught to show a waitress the same respect one shows a CEO, yeah, I guess I am. It isn't just my democratic indignation that is causing me heartburn. I believe that, as a manager, I am responsible for being a leader who shows justice and fairness to their people. I am, and should be, held to a higher standard because I'm a leader.

I find myself "imprinting" on the Chinese, like a duckling who is raised with puppies and thinks, 'I'm a puppy, not a duckling.' All day long I see their beautiful, white, soft skin that makes them look 20 years younger than they actually are, and as I wash my hands in the bathroom, I see my Caucasian face in the mirror and think, 'Who's the old white woman?'

One adventure I am emphatic about avoiding is purchasing a car in Malaysia. Dave has been planning to work this out with a new acquaintance, Vittoria, who is on her way back to Rome. But Dave falls ill from, we suspect, eating at a hawker stall.

Hawker stalls are like US food courts, except that they're outside and clean with boiling water instead of Lysol. They have great, cheap food and you can get almost anything you want that isn't Tex-Mex or grain-fed steak. However, *some* people with delicate GI tracts should *not* eat their way down the left side of the menu...thank you very much, Dave!

We agree to buy Vittoria's Perodua Kembara, a small four-door "high wagon," sometimes known as a "cute ute," or cute utility vehicle. I insist on calling it a "kookaburra" after the Australian bird known both for its crazy laugh and for killing snakes by dropping them from a high perch or battering them senseless with their big bills. I call it that so often that I forget the true name of the car.

So, during a very stressful week, I go alone to the motor vehicle department to complete the purchase. Rafeeq, my driver, has agreed to help me as interpreter. He texts me when he arrives at our apartment building and we head out at 7:30am, me following him. We arrive before 8:00am and stand as close to the door as I think is reasonable to hold our place in line. A local comes and stands between me and the door.

I've been in this country long enough to know it's okay to take back the first place in line by moving in front of him, closer to the door. He does not care at all and moves back to second in the queue. I do not give him a lecture in line etiquette as some of my Australian and British friends have a habit of doing. There's no need.

Once inside, I exchange the title to the car and pay the fees. Rafeeq has to speak with uniformed officers to help things go smoothly, and while he does, I get this far away feeling and a strong surge of emotion. Huge, salty tears fill my eyes.

I am so thankful for Rafeeq and his daily help. Even though I pay him for his services, I am still struck by how utterly helpless I would be in this place without kind people like him. I wipe the tears away, unashamed, but need to get out of there and back to work. It is beautifully sunny and lovely, just as it was during my site visit months before. In the 10:00am light, the road to the office looks so much more inviting than at 7:00am.

But as I near the Nocura building, I realize I've been here

for 23 days, and the quicksand is forming around my ankles. Why did I have to push so hard to come here?

I think I'm going a little crazy. So, I write to my best friend.

-----Original Message-----
To: Tara
From: Janna
Subject: RE: So glad it's time to write, again.
I am in a heap of trouble here, I have to tell you.
My team is making mistakes, people are quitting left and right and I don't want to work the 12-hour days it's going to take to fix it.
Please pray for me. I don't feel like I can be honest with anyone about how I feel, after how I wrote so cheerfully and full of faith about my first week.
I was so vulnerable when I wrote that, not protecting myself. Well, there's a whole lot of bad stuff going on that people are laying at my doorstep and if I don't get worried, they're just going to be up in my face harder.
I love you, just didn't think I'd regret coming here so hard or so fast. Can't tell my Mom, don't want others to be sad for me.

I received an email back from Tara telling me about Dylan, a friend of ours who was sentenced to a year in prison. Never thought I'd write that about a friend. Dylan worked in the financial services industry. It seems some mistakes were made by employees in his company, Dylan included. This was innocently reported by the new planner in the office to an inquisitive SEC rep. Now, after months of prayer and pleading with God by so many people, Dylan must be made an example and will spend a year in federal prison. I promise to write him there. I'm going on a journey of my own and know what it's like to mark time and hide in shame.

-----Original Message-----
From: Tara
To: Janna Donovan
Subject: Hey!
Hopefully you are in a restful sleep while I write this--juicin' up for another taxing, but rewarding and productive week. Maybe I had some hard, lonely times so that I could better support Dylan who had some grim news to bear this week after being sentenced to 1 year in a federal correctional institute. Lot of Jesus and a little Holy spirit are helping him through. Going to send him off with some journals like yours.
You asked about emailing him. I don't know if Dylan can get email. He'll give me all the info--it could be Connecticut, Pennsylvania, West Virginia or Kentucky. He's really hoping for West Virginia so his boys can visit more often. Stomach ache. I'll keep you posted.
The stronger the current rushes over us, the more interesting the shape of the rock--Tara's translation. Love you, miss you!
Thank you for remaining my running partner despite the vast ocean(s)!!!
Love, me

I continue to try to think of others—something I've been taught to do when I feel down. Friends. Friends of friends. And, of course, my husband whom I love so much. I send Dave an email full of cheer and happiness, telling him to eat right and take care of himself. He responds.

-----Original Message-----
From: David Donovan
To: Janna Donovan
Subject: Hi, hope you're doing better
I'm doing just that, having a frappuccino at starbucks as I type, you know lots of carbs, protein and caffeine, all the important nutrition for a growing boy. Thanks for thinking of me. I love you Janna. Thanks for a great adventure.
DaveD

I meet with Ian, the head of Server and Connectivity Marketing. Ian is a mensch if there ever was one. Or, if you like, "salt of the earth" in Texan. He is professional and that does not get in the way of him being friendly. He knows how to explain situations to executives and understands how things work at Nocura. He always has timely jokes and a smile for the situation, and he seems to handle the whole work-life balance thing very well.

I show Ian my list of "critical few." At any moment, Nocura employees are supposed to know their top two or three focus projects that will make an immediate impact. Of course, my list is ten items long. He immediately says, "You need to learn how to say no. You need to learn how to push back. State the list of what you can do and only work on those things."

Easy for him to say. He's been here two years. I walk out, thinking, 'How do I say no to Juliana? It just isn't that easy. I owe it to her to say yes.'

Chapter 5
AUGUST IN THE RED

Monday, August 1, 2005 - Penang, Malaysia

It is the first month of the quarter and profits are down, so we've been given fresh orders from top Asia management to raise our prices in *all* markets. But August sales start off painfully slow. Daily status meetings become a sea of red, the color that shows all our low-performing metrics. We're drowning. Emails with our results are flashed several times a day for all execs in Asia to see, regardless of whether the news is bad or good.

Our Brand Analyst, who's been putting in nights and weekends for several months, takes leave during the first week of August. That leaves me and the Print Advertising Manager to analyze the products and pricing with the goal of getting our sales jumpstarted. We quickly realize that, even if we lower prices to spur demand, our efforts will not begin to show results until the third and fourth weeks of the month.

The direct mail brochure cannot be changed and will just sit on our customers' desks with its higher prices all month long.

My boss, Juliana, is also on leave, so two other directors step in to help us do some reactionary price planning. I am painfully new to many of the concepts they are reeling off.

On Wednesday of that first week, people at the top of the chain are calling and asking what actions we are taking to bring the call volume back up. They seemingly ignore the fact that any changes we make won't go to press until the middle of the following week. All we can do is watch each hour pass as the red continues to be emailed out. No amount of calling and complaining is going to change that.

I am furious. Didn't it all start with their request that we increase margins by raising prices in an extremely price-sensitive market?

I feel like the rabble-rousers in the movie *The Big Easy*. The police come to their poor neighborhood to investigate a drug murder that the officers do not realize has been committed by one of their own. An angry mob gathers outside the crack house and yells, "Don't look at us! Ya'll did it!"

I am not just embarrassed because the results are bad on my watch. I am angry for *my* people who left it all on the field in the previous quarter, only to have people think they are complete idiots because they followed our hopeful direction. I don't want to be a captain who does this to their soldiers. I have been taught that, to be a manager, one of the most important qualities you demonstrate is courage. You spread the credit when things go right. You take all the blame when things go wrong.

But my team seems to expect the blame that is cast on them. They stand there and take it. They make me feel naïve and silly for "sticking up for them," which I do, but only feebly.

It's not quite *Office Space* with directors over-managing analysts about coversheets on TPS reports. But it does feel like we need to see our blind spots or lead differently. How do we show them more accurately what goes on in our own division? The company may just be too big.

Given our size and lack of visibility, how do we help execs hear from the people who could give them the true story? Is the problem an over-respect for the ranks above us? Is no one below allowed to speak up?

Do we think that people asking questions or disagreeing will slow down the decision-making process too much? Is it possible that they do not know how much their decisions affect the goals they are shouting at us for not achieving?

Of course, leaders can't be expected to predict the future. They are risk-takers. They throw the spaghetti on the wall and hope something sticks. But could they have argued this out at the top before sending the decision down to us? Which is more important: sales volume or margin?

I and my team, overworked and over-worried, wonder how to achieve these two competing goals. If everything is a priority, it seems like nothing is a priority. So, we just work harder and try to achieve both goals. We stay later and later, and I tell myself that Dave and Sean are just going to have to understand.

I've only been here a month and it feels like the wheels are falling off. I remember reading an article in *The National Geographic* about crab fisherman in the Bering Sea. The perils and demands of their work included injuries, working non-stop around the clock, and the ever-present possibility of being swept overboard. I finished the article, exhausted from just reading it, and find out they'd only been on the boat for eight days. Not trying to be dramatic here, just saying this thing has gone downhill fast.

"Embrace the suck," I tell myself. "Get over it!"

Friday, August 5, 2005

While I'm struggling at work, I learn that Sean isn't faring so well either. He is having all sorts of trouble at school. After a class field trip, he is sent to the principal's office for being disruptive and swearing. He says he was repeating what he heard other boys say. We hear a rumor from another parent that classmates are also accusing and blaming Sean for things they do, and he ends up being the one who takes the blame. His teacher acknowledges as much and shows me some clever ways to address it with his fellow students when it happens.

In addition to that, the faculty and principal arrange an ISE (independent student education) program that requires more attention to his behavior.

I am immediately self-conscious that others will think he learned to swear at home because we are American, that we are low brow and unable to parent properly. But why do I immediately go there? I am so enamored with the idea of this opportunity for Sean that I am not thinking about how hard the changes are for his seven-year-old brain and body. We've brought Sean here to give him a rigorous International Baccalaureate education and expand his cultural horizons, but it seems that, like us, he is just struggling with the move. I want to give him this gift and I desperately want it to work out.

It is ironic. The thing that most attracted us to the Penang International School was that the children are allowed the freedom to act like kids when they are not in class. At Sean's school in Houston, I felt that they marched them to class single file, asked them to speak in hushed tones at lunch, and allowed less time for play outside. I feared that, at any moment, the school might mandate that I medicate this super high-energy boy or else.

But at Uplands he has been given this sprawling, secured campus with lush lawns where he is asked to manage himself instead of being highly controlled and monitored by adults. At lunchtime, he is free to run around for the entire hour or, if he remembers to go, attend one of the many clubs and activities. I think maybe he is surprised and almost giddy at the amount of freedom he has and is not managing himself well.

Daniel Worth, Sean's principal, tells me one of the most important strengths in Sean is intellectual curiosity. He predicts that this will keep Sean moving onward and upward toward academic success.

But Sean still has to learn to manage his emotions, organize himself without complaining, and not speak until he's engaged his brain. How many times have I heard that advice? Too bad he has Dave and me for examples. It's hard to teach my child about things I still struggle with. At least I can admit I'm a hypocrite. That's a little bit better than not acknowledging it at all, right?

Enough with the insecurity, fault-finding, and theories. On to practical solutions! Dave works with Mr. Worth to help Sean's transition go more smoothly and writes me an email to keep me in the loop.

-----Original Message-----
From: Dave Donovan
To: Janna Donovan
Subject: Have a nice day!
Just wanted to tell you things went well with Mr. Worth. He will instigate an ISE? independent student education for Sean. Mr. Worth was very sympathetic to Sean and his situation and felt that Sean would respond well when given extra attention. I am meeting with Mr. W again Thursday at 8.00 after he has met with the teacher's that interact with Sean to review the plan. Then we will implement email follow up between me and the teachers. There will be another review in 6 weeks.

Just before I left I asked an aside regarding Rugby which Mr. W went into a 30 min. discussion over. He is passionate about his rugby. I'll fill you in on the details later.

Kick their asses, take names and come home early :-)
Jumpa lagi, DaveD

When I slow down the worrying about my seven-year-old son, I go back to worrying about my team and my numbers. When the details become too much to handle, I find myself going to the bathroom to take a break, cry, or just be alone with no one asking me questions. Never thought I'd write that sentence, let alone be lame enough to do it.

Wednesday, August 17, 2005

Back home in our Penang high rise, some mornings I awake and instantly get mad that I survived the night. 'I'm still in the nightmare. How do I get out of this unscathed?' I think. I entertain elaborate fantasies of lying down by the fireplace at

Mom and Darrel's in New Mexico after a long day in the snow. Escape fantasies are powerful stuff when you are entering a dark place, whether it's vague thoughts of disappearing from the planet, or hiding out at Mom's.

A bright spot appears when our house in the US sells and the deal closes. Yeah! We get a sweet financial reward for 12 years of blood, sweat, and a lot of tears that went into completely rebuilding our house. Dave replaced everything but the front door and the brick fireplace. He was exhausted and glad to be rid of it. But my joy is bittersweet because that stupid house was our tie to Texas. Now we have no place we can go back to when we've completed our time here.

The entire ownership of that house had been a test of our relationship. Five years into our marriage, after a lot of hard work, planning, and living on only one salary, we retired from our jobs. We bought the place, stored our things, and set about traveling the world for five years. All was going according to plan. But in between trips to Prague and Santiago and the Caribbean, we set about repairing this little duplex. It was more of a mess than we'd bargained for, so our main motivation became the desire to not be slumlords when we finally did rent it.

The only tool we should have used was a bulldozer. We argued about it a lot.

Finally, the traveling came to an end, and I desperately wanted the house finished. I also wanted to have a child. Dave said, "Both of these things can become a reality, but one of us has to go back to work. You know, a child needs full insurance, not our catastrophic, high deductible kind." He also said, "If we have a child, I'd like to be the one who stays home with him. My dad was gone most weeks on business trips. I want to know my son." So, I heard the "one of us" as "Janna" and set about firing up the job-finding network.

A friend, Liam, who Dave had worked with in Tokyo several years prior, had gathered a solid team and started a dot-com. The dot-com was selling through VARs (Value Added Resellers), who were solo consultants that provided hands-on setup or consulting to small businesses. It was 1995, and everyone was interested in how a startup called Amazon was managing to sell books online.

Several phone calls and conversations were had and I interviewed at the dot-com. They offered me a job and I thought, 'Whatever it takes to finish the house, right?

Sean was born at home one year later, and my CEO and President encouraged me to work from home for the next 20 months. Dave was a natural stay-at-home dad, far more patient and concerned with nutritious meals than I ever would have been. During this time, friends and relatives would always ask when our home was going to be finished, but our marriage was more important than our stupid house. I decided to just quit arguing about it.

Five years later, our dot-com ran out of runway, even with $40 million in annual revenue. It was sold to a California super-VAR and only retained 5 of its 130 employees, so I attempted to get a consulting business off the ground. After a lackluster year and only five clients, I gave in and asked friends to help me get an interview at Nocura. I interviewed for a month, and suddenly I was in. I was immediately shocked by the culture of high tech. Working for Nocura seemed like trying to please wealthy, strict parents who rarely hand out lavish praise or approval. But I was also happy there. I loved my teammates, learned to deliver, and

Dave finished reconstructing the duplex. Problem solved.

We only had two years in that fully rebuilt home of ours, and now here we are in Malaysia with a new set of hopes and dreams. Without the burden of house remodeling every weekend, we want to have more fun and build a good life while we're here in Penang. We want to think of ways to connect each day, to relax together, to go on regular dates each week. We want to show Sean a big, wide world and make a home for him in it. We want him to learn how to get out and live life, not talk about it or play a video game that simulates it.

We want to hang pictures and buy plants and stock the fridge for guests. We want to stay in touch with friends in Texas with Skype and instant messaging. I want to deepen our faith and our understanding of God and His grace. All of these things require energy. I have to set some boundaries with Nocura and spend time at home once in a while.

Yet, I have big dreams at work too. I want to be honest, positive, and enthusiastic. I want to understand the numbers, ask questions constantly, and lead the team in achieving results.

The thought of balancing all these things in Malaysia makes my stomach turn with the weight of it. I want so much for me and my family, and I'm achieving none of it.

I am homesick. There is no doubt. Who knew football would be a huge trigger? It is not "next to" religion in Texas. It *is* religion. I remember my grandfather greeting our preacher at the back of the church after the service ended. He'd tap his watch and say, "Need to get home for game time."

Now, on Sundays in Malaysia, Dave's favorite thing to do is to listen to college football broadcast via radio on his PC.

The college games take place on Saturdays in the States, but that's Sunday here.

Sitting in the other room, I can hear every local radio ad for cars and insurance and some of my favorite post-game restaurants. But instead of giving me great joy, the nostalgia drives me out of the apartment with tears in my eyes. I can't stand to listen to the familiar sounds, and I know I'm not alone in this. My Canadian pastor, who is a hockey fan, says he chokes up when he hears the theme music for NHL games. Sports...who knew?

I'm homesick for my parents, anything Texan, actually anything *Tex-Mex*. But football must be the symbol in my mind for everything American. Elegant violence, love for your teammates above all else, poor kids making good on promises to buy their mom a big house, and strong farm boys held back as little six-year-olds so they'll be bigger when they play as high school freshmen. Taking Sean to Ricky Williams' Heisman parade down Congress Avenue in Austin, Bart Starr's smashed face, Vince Lombardi in the Ice Bowl. And who can forget Sean's favorite player, Louisiana's favorite son, Brett Favre.

While I'm homesick, Dave and Sean are having a pretty good time. I want to enjoy this with them! I think Dave sees that I'm struggling, so he sends me constant support, trying to prop me up before I get too low.

-----Original Message-----
From: David Donovan
To: Janna Donovan
Subject: sean says
This morning on the way (driving) to school sean offered the

following: maybe the cars cost so much here (i think he said "the extra thousand" - being the diff between what we sold the honda for and what we paid for the cookooburro) because they come with the beautiful view of Penang. I agreed.
Jumpa lagi nanti
DaveD

-----Original Message-----
From: David Donovan
To: Janna Donovan
Subject: Thanks
Janna
Thanks for the opportunity to live a world away. Thanks for the chance to fix my mind and body. Thanks for taking me along with you. Days like this remind me of why we did this. I am smiling big time. I love you. This is making a difference in the life of a boy struggling with growing up, stuck somewhere between his earthly desires and his heavenly aspirations. Probably important for Sean too :-).
Jumpa lagi nanti

I write to a friend in Houston who works for Nocura. He's always been a trusted confidante.

-----Original Message-----
From: Janna Donovan
To: Derek Hunt
Cc: David Donovan
Subject: It's hard, miss you

Thought about you at your reunion, hope it was a good time between friends. Hope the school year has gotten off to a great start! How are the "boys" + 1 new daughter?

Haven't wanted to write again because I didn't want ya'll to worry.

I love the people I work with but I have to grit my teeth about 14 times a day to keep from fully admitting, "Right now, I hate my job" (then something goes right and I feel silly for hating it.)

Hard to read emails from friends at work because I go soft and right now I kind of need to be hard, making high dollar decisions, not glamorous as you know. :o)

Found a great little church, not many people but mostly expats with all different backgrounds.

Even sold our house already for 3x what we paid for it!!!!!!!!

Lots of stuff to smile about and look forward to, just homesick. Besides you and some other friends, you know what I miss most? MEXICAN FOOD!

Love you both, take care, see you soon!
Janna

-----Original Message-----
From: Derek Hunt
To: Janna Donovan
Cc: David Donovan
Subject: RE: It's hard, miss you
Hey Janna and Dave,
Great to hear from you!

The boys are mostly doing great. They were here last week, so I took a couple of days off for the visit. The youngest made the best grades last semester (spring) at College of any student!!!!! And just found out that he made all A's during the summer session. He's taking 20 hours this fall and applying at State and a bigger school in Business - eCommerce.

The oldest got promoted to the sales dept at his Toyota dealership, and has sold 8 cars in his first three weeks. We celebrated by buying a Toyota Prius (the Hybrid Electric Car) from him last week – which makes me a Tree Huggin' Redneck – aren't you glad you know one?????

Hang in there with work – if it's any consolation, things aren't a lot happier in the US. Revenue misses make things that way – at least your region is leading the pack in the revenue dept!!!!!!! I personally think it's because they have you there.

Glad to hear your house sold so quickly – it's a beautiful place – Dave you really did an incredible job on it, and now you get to reap the benefits! That's awesome.

We have 12 members of the Nocura Asia team coming from Aug 22 – Sep 2. Not only do we have to complete Planning for our project in two weeks, we have to entertain these folks breakfast / lunch / dinner / weekends for two weeks. There is a lot of arguing between the US and Asia teams that has built over the last three months, and now we get to live together for two weeks – I am so looking forward to Labor Day weekend!!!!!!!!

Well that's all for now – give Sean a big hug for us, and thanks for keeping in touch.

We still love and miss you guys

Monday, August 29, 2005 – Our 18th Wedding Anniversary

I leave right in the middle of a planning meeting for September pricing to celebrate my anniversary with Dave at Bagan Restaurant. We enjoy a good meal and several drinks and then take a cab home for a private anniversary celebration. I am so happy, mostly because I haven't let Dave down like I have several times in the last two months. I actually came home when I said I would. Seems like a first.

I must say, being crazy has made for some great sex with my husband. I am, of course, clinging to him for dear life during the day. But I am demanding and initiating with him, even if I get home late. I see a little fear in his eyes when I'm so desperate. I'm not saying he doesn't enjoy it; I'm just saying he doesn't know what to think. But anniversary sex is tender and loving and has an "I'm gonna be here no matter what" quality to it.

Hurricane Katrina strikes New Orleans, but I cannot watch any of the footage. I feel devastated for the people but can't bring myself to look at the photos. So many triggers to cry, to miss the US. I don't have any room left in my heart.

Princess Diana comes to mind for some odd reason. She died on our anniversary, I think. Little black cloud over us? C'mon, suit up and show up! And, since I'm from Texas, hair up and makeup! Got to stop focusing on the negative.

But it's very hard to switch it off.

Chapter 6
INDEPENDENCE FROM WHAT?

Tuesday, August 30 - Penang, Malaysia - Merdeka Day

We all have the day off in the middle of the week to celebrate Malaysia's independence from British rule. Dave and Sean and I go to the top of our four-story car park to play tennis. We warm up with ground strokes, net play, and lobs. As we begin to play a real game, I cannot shut off a tape that is playing in my head.

"Janna, you cannot do this. You are such a loser. You don't really have any will to win. You're all show and no go. This is all your fault. All of it."

My heart begins to pound, and my breath becomes short. I feel like someone has punched me right in the stomach and is now sitting on my chest. I have to sit down courtside in the afternoon sun. Am I having a heart attack? If not, it's the worst panic attack so far.

I look over at the four-story hospital across the street

from our building and I tell Dave I have to do something. I shower and, with my hair still wet, I walk into the plush hospital lobby, sobbing. In the Emergency Room, I tell them I cannot calm down. They begin asking questions. I tell them things I haven't told anyone. About how ashamed I feel for not being able to do my job, about how I've thought that disappearing (suicide) would fix the situation. I tell them I don't want anyone at work to know I've been here. They set up appointments with the staff psychologist and a psychiatrist at another hospital. Then they give me some anti-anxiety medication.

I take it and return home to lie in front of the television.

This fear is uncharacteristic of me. I have always been the one in my family and group of friends with a lot of fight. Fearless. Jump-off-the-bridge-before-everyone-else, swim in the Pacific Ocean with 200 barracuda kind of reckless.

"Why am I acting like this?" I ask. There is no rhyme or reason for this reaction. It's made worse because I have always thought of myself as the strong, hero type. Not weak and overwhelmed by reasons that have no explanation.

I survived being frightened when I was a child. When someone crashed my private boundary, it made me a little mean, but I survived. My awareness of situations and how to deal with them has protected me.

But here, in a foreign country, I am becoming more aware of everything. At times, my body tenses up, my blood pumps, and I breathe fast. The fight or flight response kicks in when I don't want or need it to. Let's just say I have a lot of marbles in the bag marked 'The world is a dangerous place and people can't be trusted', and it's getting in the way of my ability to function. Tense shoulders, heaviness on my chest, shivers. I want to get out of wherever I am.

I guess this is just the way it is in the Big Leagues. I have had anxiety and fear back in the US, and this is just another level because I've reached up. Everyone else who's playing at this level tells me I have to leave the island of Penang once a quarter to survive.

I analyze my anxiety as a way to live with it. The same things make me panic here as they did back home:

- Lack of listening
- People who do not pull their weight (now that's me)
- Constant change
- Not being trained
- Not enough resources to do what I am being asked

I went to a university that placed courage and loyalty above every other character trait I could ever hope to develop. Our student center was ringed with plaques of military men who'd won the Congressional Medal of Honor. Whether on the battlefield or the football field, we were inspired by tough people who played hurt, laid down their lives for their friends, and fought for the guy next to them.

But my war and American football analogies only mean something to me. Would anyone here understand?

One more reason to feel alone.

Besides, those men and women were truly involved in war. Nothing I'm going through is life-threatening. So why am I so overwhelmed and physically battered by the situation I find myself in? This thought just leads me to turn on myself even harder.

Wednesday, August 31, 2005

The new head of Nocura CAC and our South Asia VP are on their way to Penang to attend a performance review tomorrow morning.

In the past, I've dealt pretty well with execs. In previous jobs, I've been close to the people who sign my paycheck, monitor my results, and control the flow of money. As a financial analyst I reported to a Controller and Executive VP. In another job as an IT business analyst, I was the right hand to my Chief Information Officer. I have constantly interacted with execs, so I have a lot of confidence doing it. I genuinely like many of them. I think I've been smart in how I interact, and I've shown genuine respect, even if I felt they didn't deserve it.

This makes me think about father figures and their impact on how I deal with authority.

Unlike me, my husband's dad and friends' fathers were high-achieving executives and officers in the military. Whether daughter or son, many followed in their footsteps and did what it took to be included and recognized first by their dads, and eventually by their bosses.

Others went the other way and suffered "Mighty Oak Syndrome," where huge, mature trees block the sunlight from reaching the young, small trees on the forest floor. Those friends didn't get a lot of light, or a lot of chances to build self-confidence. In those relationships, there was a lot of criticism and less connection.

Another friend had a father who was a middle-class guy, steady but cautious, passive and unmotivated. My friend felt like he had to raise his dad or, at least, protect him. My friend was resentful because he wanted a certain kind of success, but didn't have a line of sight to it, or a clear example on how to achieve it. He had to pedal twice as fast to get half as far in business. He was angry that people got promoted because of who they knew, and he was jealous that other men and women had already experienced so much because of who their fathers were. Meanwhile, he felt stuck doing more work, hoping that what he did was good enough to be noticed for a promotion.

I honestly don't know how each of my different father figures affected how I deal with authority. Who influenced me to judge bosses who I deem aloof, out of touch, and unconcerned? If I see evidence that my bosses are unapproachable, all further evidence confirms my opinion. So, for these types, I try to stay just out of their reach and under their radar. I find the answers on my own and grumble behind their back about their lack of attention to my projects.

Do I half expect leaders to disappoint me? I anticipate harsh criticism even when my goals have been met. However, if I am distrustful and dismissive, it's never to their face. I am afraid to ask questions when something is not clearly articulated or supported with the right resources. I want to appear tough and strong, even if I can't truly be. So, I don't ask.

To be fair, I have memories of good bosses who are like my dad. After I turned six years old, my parents divorced. I spent Wednesdays and every other weekend with my father. He is someone who blusters and shouts and criticizes but also has a good sense of humor and is always game for fun.

A man who was my stepfather for 10 years was a key authority figure from elementary school until my senior year in high school. He struggled with alcohol. He taught me that rules without relationship breed rebellion in me. He demanded more out of me than he demanded out of himself. Mixed messages, blame, and criticism were the norm. Even while his own life was falling apart, he spent much of his time criticizing what I was like or what I was doing. I wasn't comfortable inviting friends over because I didn't know what he'd say, or how much we'd argue.

My brothers, Jim and John, had a way better relationship with him, while I was ready to think the worst of him and him of me. He wasn't into anything illegal like one friend's dad, but I wanted no part of his lifestyle and worked very hard to not become like him.

In some way, I am still working in my mind to change him, or, at least, show him how wrong he was. I guard this secret from friends at work and home. I think it makes me fight and grind harder.

Thursday, September 1, 2005

The Nocura division head and our South Asia VP arrive for the performance review. I am concerned that my team will not be in the meeting to answer the important detailed questions that will inevitably arise.

This is my doing. I relieved them of their "big meeting" duties so they could focus on the real work at hand. Now I am the only one from my team in the meeting, and it's scaring the crap out of me.

In the past, I had so little respect for bosses who couldn't answer questions from execs without their subordinates in the room. Sitting in this meeting, I suddenly realize why they needed us. Someone who manages lots of people can't and shouldn't know all the details of each part of the business. I had been so naïve before, thinking that my managers shouldn't have to depend on their team members to make them look smart. *Ouch.*

Adding drama to this sudden moment of revelation is the anti-anxiety pill I've taken this morning. I've never taken downers before, and I smoked pot only a handful of times when I was younger, so I have very little experience functioning while drugged. It's surreal to have two ranking execs at the head of the table and not feel worried about it one bit. In my head I am literally singing the song 'I Wanna Be Sedated' by the Ramones. Can this get any weirder?

Somehow, the meeting goes very well. Among the 25 people in the room, I get singled out by the General Manager. "Janna," she asks, "Do you have anything to add to this Thailand discussion?"

Luke has just given me information on what products Thailand needs that Nocura won't currently let them sell. They want them marketed in Thailand. Execs are always yelling at us about Thailand's dismal numbers, so I lob some product requests over the fence just to see what happens. They seem to like that suggestion, and I have a moment of fun stuck into the middle of an uptight two days. Big grin.

The following night, I go see the psychologist, Dr. Chang, a Malaysian who's ethnically Chinese and educated in New England. She is down to earth, caring, and *gets me* from the moment I walk in. She hands me a piece of paper about cognitive distortions, a pairing of words I've never heard, and says, "Are you doing any of these? Give yourself a one to ten rating."

I read over the list and hand back the paper. "Yes, I do them all, all the time," I say, laughing aloud.

"You do them *all*? All the time?" she asks, forgetting to hide her shock and surprise.

Hey, what can I say? I'm an all or nothing kind of person.

"Cognitive distortions are logical, but they are not rational," she tells me. "They can create real difficulty with your thinking. You must combat them with corrective thoughts."

"But how?" I ask.

We agree to meet regularly so she can teach me how to do that.

Sunday, September 4, 2005

At church, with the anxiety meds taking hold and the stress numbed, I find it hard to listen. So, I write in the little pink notebook that GreatHopeGals gave me. On the cover it says, "The Best is Yet to Bee" with flowers and bees on the front.

"God, I'm not mad at You. I'm mad at me. I knew this was going to be hard on work-life balance. I see all kinds of mercies from You, every morning. I just don't want this to rip me away from You. If I don't get good, will they send me away? Gotta think of others. Gotta step up out of this trench I'm in and stop digging.

What about the things I thought we'd do together here? What about the prisoners I wanted to help? Help me love me more. Help Sean love Sean more. Help Dave love Dave more.

Am I doing it Your way? That's all I ask. I just can't tell. There are so many voices to listen to, so much advice. I'm confused! Show me how to "be strong and do the work." Not out of competition. Out of faith, out of closeness to You. I belong to You as a slave redeemed from the auction block. Help me not to think red automatically means I'm not doing Your will. I will rethink the fact that red is the worst thing that can happen.

Teach me to do Your will, for You are my God. Let Your good spirit lead me on level ground.

I'm not mad at You, I'm mad at me."

During these times I take more comfort in the dark parts of the Bible than the bright, joyful ones. Case in point—Psalms 102 and 109:

"Lord; … Do not hide your face…
I groan aloud and am reduced to skin and bones.
I lie awake; I have become like a bird alone on a roof…
I eat ashes as my food and mingle my drink with tears."

"… Lord, … out of the goodness of your love, deliver me. For I am poor and needy, and my heart is wounded within me…My knees give way from fasting; my body is thin and gaunt. I am an object of scorn to my accusers; when they see me, they shake their heads. Help me, Lord my God; save me according to your unfailing love."

Chapter 7
DEPRESSION COMES

My diary entries have dropped off almost completely. I just don't have the time or energy.

Monday, September 5 - September 9, 2005
(Week 10 in Penang)

I'm working harder but I don't know at what. The results just aren't there for me to look at.

I can't use my God-given talent for influence and motivation because it's buried in the chaos. I can't even get up in the morning out of love for my team.

For the first time in my life, I don't care. I'm unafraid of being fired, receiving a bad review, or scoring badly on the annual survey. I'm so exhausted I wish they would fire me so I can get some rest. Every day at work I'm terrified I'll do something irreversibly wrong, because I don't know what expenditures or decisions I'm approving amongst the 200 emails I send out daily.

-----Original Message-----
From: Janna Donovan
To: Elizabeth Thompson; Juliana Vásquez
Cc: Team
Subject: Ill today, working from home
Going to the doctor this morning.
Will be online if you need me.
Janna

-----Original Message-----
From: Chong
To: Janna Donovan
Subject: RE: Ill today, working from home
Janna,
There is nothing more important than taking care of yourself, not even the business or company. Our family needs us.
Take care.
Chong

I go to the psychiatrist's office. He is Chinese, smart, smiling, and gentle, with a voice that is very soothing. But my emotion meter registers nothing when he begins to "examine" me.

How can I tell this intellectual man how my heart hurts? How do I tell him how I used to be? I want to convince people this is not the real me, but I'm afraid of a white straitjacket.

"This is not the real me you are meeting. This person before you is someone else," I hear myself say.

They say cognitive distortions can create difficulty with your thinking, but who knew they could also wreck the rest of your body? The psychiatrist listens to me tell him what has happened to my brain, how I used to be able to remember everything and how I was the most decisive person on any team. I tell him how I don't sleep anywhere except in the car on the way to work and in the car on the way home.

He asks, "What would you say is the average number of hours of sleep you get per day?"

"*One*," I respond. I tell him how plump I used to be, but I've lost about 25 pounds. All he sees is a very thin, old-looking person. I tell him how cold I am in the building. I think back to movie theaters in the heat of a Texas summer. I usually had to take blankets. I hate being cold. He asks if I think the shaking is from being cold or being afraid. The shivering is from being cold. The shaking is from being scared.

It seems to me that he is mentally ticking off a list. Well, at least I am right about something. There *is* a list. And everyone I talk to seems to know about it, except me. I get a copy:

1. Sad, anxious, or empty mood that lasts two weeks or more
2. Loss of interest or pleasure in most activities you once enjoyed
3. Feelings of worthlessness, hopelessness, guilt
4. Difficulty concentrating or making decisions
5. Changes in sleep habits (not able to sleep or oversleeping)
6. Significant change in weight or appetite
7. Fatigue, loss of energy, feeling "slowed down"
8. Agitation, restlessness, irritability
9. Frequent thoughts of death or suicide, or suicide attempts

If I have the first two symptoms accompanied by some of the others, I am officially depressed.

I've got all nine.

What is happening to me? Why can't I just snap out of it? Nothing is truly endangering me! This truth makes my illogical self-incrimination even worse. Why am I suddenly afraid of everything? Oh my, what if I really came upon a true trauma like Dave or Sean dying? Oh, please don't go there, tired little brain. Please, give it a rest.

The doctor prescribes anti-anxiety and anti-depressant drugs. I remind him to make the dosage small because I am highly sensitive to medication. I went through an entire pregnancy and gave birth at home without so much as one aspirin. I don't take cold medicine, ever.

I ask lots of questions. Is there a reduced dosage for people like me? What if I get addicted? Is that a thing? What if I don't respond like he thinks I am going to? What if I gain a lot of weight? They say that is a side effect. I should be welcoming that at this point, but the thought of eating makes me sick.

To me, there is no scarier feeling than not being able to control myself. I know I must have felt that way a couple of other times in my life, but I have managed to erase them from my memory. Another obstacle that I don't want to admit to anyone: I believe a stereotype that committed people of faith—devoted followers of Christ—do not use medication. I thought it should not be necessary and that it's just wrong.

He just keeps smiling gently and says, "You have to give them time to work. Once you start, you cannot stop taking them for two months. That would be dangerous and could plunge you into an even deeper depression than before."

What?

After such a serious visit to the doctor, it is oddly fun to be out and about during the day, playing hooky from work.

This is more like I imagined my time in Penang would be. However, when I get back home, I turn on my laptop and read more about anti-depressants and anti-anxiety drugs.

Great gobs! I cannot believe how dangerous these things are! I do a search and immediately find so many people who've posted their bad experiences for all to see on blogs.

"Searing headache."

"Gained twenty pounds."

"Bad for your liver."

"Not worth the side effects."

"Study shows teens become suicidal, or worse, homicidal."

So many say that the medication actually made them *more* depressed. How can that be? Oh, why does every way I go seem to arrive at a dead end in the wrong part of town?

However, one guy's comment haunts me (and would for a long time afterwards): "These things are trash. I got off of them and went back to what I knew would strengthen me: *my faith*." Thank you, Christian dude. I would do that if I could, but I can't! What else you got?

I reason that to keep my job I probably need to take the drug. But the drug can hurt my liver, so I decide that no job is worth hurting my liver or worse. I have enough to deal with without becoming a fat, suicidal woman with a permanent headache. Besides, I live on the 23rd floor of this building! Don't think I haven't thought about jumping. I'm not playing. So, I pass and put the drugs way high in my closet, out of reach.

As the days roll along, triggers continue to abound.

I can't possibly get close enough to anyone to find a close female relationship. Worse, while I suffer, Dave and Sean are enjoying Penang so much and I don't want to spoil that for them. I need to talk to someone else so I don't drag them down with me.

I write and call Tara, my longtime friend, more and more frequently. Even though she is dealing with some tough things back in the US, she is a lifeline for me. Having her PhD in psychology doesn't hurt! It makes her the perfect candidate to be friends with a crazy person like me. So, I lose all pride, and refuse to fear looking pathetic. Tara and I message each other on Skype at different times of the day, even when the other one isn't there. I use our chat to let it all out:

janna: I've been trying to find friends. I have talked to God about it and said, "I just can't get it right with almost any of your daughters here in Malaysia. They are all too busy."
janna: And I then said, "You know, I think sometimes I want a close Christian friend here just because that will somehow validate me as a Christian, somehow make the picture right. I am totally intimate with 3 people: you, Dave and Mom. That is not going to change no matter where I live.
janna: So why do I have this picture in my eye that I need a "buddy" here? I guess it's because I see everyone else have one and I wonder, why not me? Why don't I have someone that saves a seat for me at church?
janna: well, partially because I never really "needed" it before?
janna: As my dad would say, "You're too damn independent for your own good."
janna: So I forget to ring someone and say, "Girrrrrrrrrrl, save me a seat."
janna: I know that highway runs BOTH ways......

janna: Or I don't say to anyone, "Girrrrrrl, I saved you a seat."
janna: My mom is like that and I told her about it last time we talked on the phone.
janna: just kinda asking if this could be one explanation for the aloneness she sometimes feels...here I am screwed up and trying to tell my Mom how to be
janna: anywho, I am so fortunate to have the healthy relationships I have and I am just through being in the business of telling God how each thing ought to be.
janna: So I was glad to examine my motives for wanting a buddy here...nobody wants to be used to complete the perfect scenario of what "janna-as-strong-christian-woman" should look like.
janna: ...they want to be loved because they need lovin'

I receive this message back from Tara. She uses some Texas twang to describe our fear as "being skeert."

-----Original Message-----
From: Tara
To: Janna Donovan
Subject: Hellloooo!!!!
Mornin',
Are you skeert?? haha.
For two chiquitas that deal with skeertness as much as we do, we still seem to do a HELL of alot of STUFF! Don't we??
I went to the T-Mobile wi-fi store today. Hoping I get the $20,000 tech grant I applied for--so I can get the communicado stuff square for the business. This is sooooooo not my a-rea! Sweet Tea in the Morning, how many more stretches do I have to do? Amazing how much I am learning, but ready for a super-sized break.

When I get the tech stuff for the business settled then I will get new stuff at home, too. Looking forward to skyping with you. Want to hear the tones in your stories, your west Texas laughter (and quivery lip if necessary.)

Took Rachel back to school yesterday. Squawled all the way home, but it was good, you know, the good of caring whether or not you are separate from someone.

Told Moma a little bit about my home strife. She said, "don't be afraid to tell me, girl...I know I can't fix it, but I know where to go to plead for your strength and wisdom." Thank you, Jesus, for Moma. She closed by saying "I know you are going to be strong in the end, I'm not worried about how you will come out, girl, just don't leave me out of helping you." So freeing to hear my mother say that.

I picture you at work. Like every time you are listening to people and trying to help them, I know you are also praying for God to show you how to best use your skill, experience and passion...even if you have to peel out on their heads a little bit (I just threw in a line that our brothers would say to make you feel at home.) hahaha.

Love your guts...with you!

Tara

Some days, I just feel better out of nowhere. Something goes right, and I manage to perform on a project with my previous fast-paced efficiency.

My next-door roommate in grad school used to have "white sock" and "black sock" days. When she was feeling strong, she'd call these "white sock" days and she'd hang a white sock out her window to let her boyfriend know it was okay to come up. She was a genius, made straight A's. Is there a connection between high intellect and depression? Must think about that later.

As soon as I feel this type of good day coming on, I write my mom or Tara and ask about them. It's like a parting of the clouds. I happily think the worst is over and that the black sock days are behind me.

-----Original Message-----
From: Janna Donovan
To: Mom
Subject: Good news, the clouds have lifted!!!!!
First, how are you? Physically, mentally? I love you and have thought about you so much. Please take care of yourself. Second, how is Darrel? Where is he in New Orleans and is he ok?
Third, the clouds have broken.
I took a day off "sick" Tuesday.
I went to a psychiatrist to get anti-depressant and anti-anxiety meds.
I went home and read a million internet posts about side effects, long-term problems like weight gain, fogginess, suicidal thoughts and that they finally had to wean themselves by exercising, no alcohol, no caffeine.
Dave has been wonderful, taking care of me, keeping the stress way low at home, staying positive. I decided this company and job were not worth trying to medicate and sedate so that I could continue like I was going. I'll give up and only do what I can do when I'm at work. If it's not good enough, it's not good enough.
(I got up Wed and Thursday and ran in the streets surrounding my apartment tower really hard, haven't done that in 10 weeks.) My boss has been telling me it IS good enough, I prayed to believe her. She's been telling me I can't do 20 other people's jobs or save them from themselves.

Got a boundary with all of them, can't make life ok for all of them. Prayed to be the nicest mean boss I could be. I realized that I was trying to be God, taking on everyone's problems, thinking I could control everything.

I told my boss that I feel like I'm not doing what's right for Nocura, making such big mistakes, potentially worth a lot of money. She said she appreciated my concern, but that's the only way to learn and we all have to make mistakes at this level.

I don't answer emails that aren't addressed directly to me (mostly). Unless someone's limb is hanging off, it doesn't go ahead of my two stated priorities. :o)

Wed and Thursday nights I slept until alarm woke me up. First in weeks.

Still not out of the woods as my newfound energy makes me want to plunge back in. So, gotta take breaks at work.

Delegate or die, that's my new motto. I'm smiling and getting back to my old self again.

Please pray I remain calm when the next big crisis hits. Please pray that I don't get back on the treadmill and try to run again like that.

Many thanks for all your prayers, thoughts, past advice, future hope, can't wait to talk to you, turn your Skype on Friday night at 6:00pm.

I LOVE YOU, MOM!
Janna

I have a good mother and several other great mother figures. My mom is extremely encouraging but may have been a little too permissive for my own good when I was young. There is always something to work out in a relationship with mothers, isn't there? Like the Freud fridge magnet says, "If it's not one thing, it's your mother."

I think I like praise at work not because I was deprived of it, but because my mother encouraged me so much. I was used to it. She did not have to challenge me; I think I was the one pushing myself.

Still, I thank God for her encouragement, warmth, forgiveness, and gratitude. I try to emulate these qualities and, believe it or not, I think they make me a good manager. Others may say, "What a kiss-up" or "Teacher's pet!" But I think it's important to know what I'm doing right. So why not tell others what they're doing right? I find this kind, positive encouragement from male bosses as often as with female bosses.

I've had people tell me I have not broken up with my mother. Maybe Mom's permissive parenting allowed me to be impulsive and self-focused with minimal rules. Her rules were never applied in a cold, harsh way, so when someone does apply rules to my life, I often see it as annoying, slowing me down, and cramping my style.

I want recognition. It's helped me work on the most important, visible projects. It's kept me from being sent to the basement with a red stapler and a feeling that I am being dismissed by everyone. I wonder if there's someone in the office who I can trust to encourage me? I know they'll challenge me, but I also need them to encourage me.

As I go back to work with a clear head, I vow to not allow last quarter's accomplishments to be overshadowed by this quarter's strategic misdirection from above. So, I go to the General Manager's admin, and I ask her to schedule a buffet lunch for Friday at the Equatorial Hotel for all 15 of my people and any other temps who support our team. When Friday finally comes, I wear the brightest lime green tank and sweater set I have along with my high heels and best earrings. With Rafeeq driving, I work on the icebreaker in the car on the way over. Each person is going to get a card with a question on it.

"What was your nickname when you were young?"

"If you were a car, what would you be?"

"Do you play a musical instrument?"

"What did you dream of being when you were a kid?"

I laugh to myself that this may be the least professional, most American activity I've done since I arrived.

We all get our first course and sit down, half of us on each side of a long table with a red tablecloth. 'We look like a big family,' I think. When each person stands up to answer their question, I can tell they love it. They laugh and cat call one another. They applaud my childhood nickname (my dad made my name seem Spanish by calling me Juanita).

Before we leave, I call them all over to a beautiful pool surrounded by large palm trees and green vegetation. I speak loudly over the waterfall rushing into the pool from the lobby above. "I just want to let you know that you are an amazing group of people. You are smart and strong. You are the reason I go to work every day." They surprise me with an award "Best Marketing Director Ever." I am so embarrassed that I'm speechless at first. Eventually, I say, "You can give me that in a year," and I shake my fist at them in mock irritation. "Okay, back to work. Lots more rows to hoe!"

At moments like these, I know in my heart that I am *not* "all hat and no cattle" no matter what the crazy little voices in my head are telling me. I am not pathetic, even though it may seem that way to some.

A week into September, we're given the final report for August. As we're all painfully aware of, it ended the same way it began: in a sea of red. We miss revenue and margin goals by a significant amount. With so much of our demand depending on the business brochure that is lying "dormant" because it's severely over-priced, we never recover those sales. Oy vey.

Random thoughts come over me as I try to push away the red flashing across my computer screen every hour.

It's weird to be in a country with no Jewish influence or culture. I had no idea that I'd notice it, much less miss it. But I do. Since Malaysia has no diplomatic ties with Israel, there's no temple, no rabbis, no Jewish symbols, no Hanukkah, and, saddest of all, no bagels. It's always about the food with me.

I still use the Yiddish phrases I learned from my mom's long-time friend: schlep, schmuck, mensch, tchotchkes, oy vey. Sean has picked them up too. At school, I hear Sean's entire third grade class of Brits, Asians and Australians say "Oy vey" when someone smacks them or does something embarrassing.

Ditto with Hispanic and Black culture, humor, food, and music. Do Americans realize how much they love the food, music, and expressions by non-WASP people? Do they take these for granted? Haven't those in the minority population of each society produced incredible food, art, poetry, and beauty? They have and still do, often with much less.

Along with the August report in red, I also receive my annual review from Juliana. I'm all nerves when I take her phone call.

To my surprise, Juliana tells me she's been impressed with my ability to shift from my role in Nocura US driving mobile phone sales into CAC marketing. She tells me, in the nine short weeks I've been here, that I've actually *met* my key deliverables, and I've brought structure and accountability to the team. I'm surprised to hear this.

What she is most impressed with, however, is that I've taken ownership of the previous negative Employee Survey results that were no fault of my own. She appreciates how I've worked with the team to correct and improve upon these results, even though I feel I haven't made nearly enough headway.

Moreover, I am impressed that Juliana understands I'm up against a steep learning curve, and though she makes it clear that she wants to see me take the next step and increase my focus on the critical few, I feel listened to, even if I don't believe everything she has to say.

She ends the call by saying I would have her full support as I work to build a successful team and business. When she hangs up, I'm surprised to find that I'm happy with my first overseas performance review.

But I have a secret.

I've started keeping 'hash-marks' in my little pink book. It was originally meant to hold the names of new friends and manicurists in Penang, but that changed a few weeks back. Now I keep a page that counts off the number of weeks I've worked in Nocura Malaysia. One-two-three-four, and then a diagonal stroke across the set denoting five weeks. It's like what you'd see on a prison wall.

I know it's a little melodramatic, but every month I hang on, that's less of the moving fee I have to pay back. I have a substantial claw back clause in my contract. Every month I stay, the amount goes down. Dylan, my friend in prison, should be the one marking his time in this way, not me. But this is something that I doggedly continue to do. Even the solid review does not reason me out of it.

Even recognition has lost its sway with me.

Chapter 8
HOLDING ON TIGHT

Saturday, September 10, 2005 - Penang, Malaysia

I'm trying to understand my symptoms. Social anxiety is the name given to that unnerving feeling that some people get when they get panicked in a social situation with no logical or apparent threat. I had heard about social anxiety when my friend's son had a panic attack right after graduating from a very prestigious college.

It's hard to describe it, so how about an example?

You are just sitting there at dinner with friends and family, and everyone is chatting and passing the salt. All is perfectly normal, but you feel like your skin is about to peel off. You want to stand up and scream at everyone to stop leaving you out of the conversation, even when they aren't. Things seem more important than they actually are. You want them to stop treating serious things so flippantly when it's truly just a light-hearted conversation.

What I had on the rooftop, playing tennis, was a panic attack. What I have when I'm at a party is social anxiety. The situations are not life-threatening, but the danger feels very real and is capable of changing my blood pressure.

Friday, September 16, 2005

This particular Friday afternoon, it is nice to be winding down and heading home. We have been asked to an evening of Trivia Games at the local Club of the Royal Australian Air Force, also known as the "Hostie." We want to get out and meet people and have a great time. This is perfect.

At about 4:00pm, our financial manager, Lilly, comes to my desk and asks me for our team's projection of how much revenue we can win back in September after the August debacle. She asked Luke for it on Wednesday but has not received it. She tells me she has to have it before we leave for the day and Luke has already left for his home several hours away to see his parents.

In the past, I've known my businesses and helped build the models that predict this kind of information down to the daily amount. I've known the numbers well enough to logically make an educated guess that I could easily give to execs and ethically stand behind. All businesspeople learn to produce an accurate "seat of the pants" estimate based on as much truth as they know at the time.

With so many markets under my command, and so little experience with them, I feel like I've just gotten a pop quiz when I haven't been to class the entire semester. I hate this feeling of helplessness. It doesn't matter if Lilly comes back in five minutes or two hours, I will be no closer to an answer that is factual. The earnings gap in August was so severe that I know it will be impossible to claw back those losses. It's not gonna happen.

I decide to just look busy and leave at 6:00pm. Lilly does not have her answer, but she also does not have a lie. How lame am I becoming? I don't know how to live with this level of lameness.

We first go to a party for new members of our church. There, I talk far too long about my own transition problems to Jennifer, an American friend, who had success in business back in the US. Our host, Craig, says, "Is there a great deal of macho energy at Nocura? Perhaps it's difficult for a woman to break into, especially in Asia?" He's just making conversation, but I want to contradict him and flippantly say, "Oh, many of my bosses at Nocura have been female. Both here and in the States."

Why am I so defensive? Why don't I want him to label the push-at-all-costs tendency at Nocura as a male thing? Why be a jerk to him? He is a guy for goodness sake, just trying to find a way to sympathize! I decide there's no time to ponder that right now. I will have to think about it another time.

We head over to the Australian Hostie by taxicab. I get there and our group is already seated and competing in an intense Trivia game. The rest of the world seems to take these things much more seriously than Americans do. Are we forever stuck in the "cool kid" syndrome from high school? Can't be nerdy or know too much!

My general manager arrives with a friend and I pull up some extra chairs. As I sit enjoying a 100-Plus isotonic drink, I realize I cannot stop my leg from shaking. All I can think about is that stupid number for Lilly and the Finance team and how it's really the general manager, Liz, right across from me who asked for it.

Mental note to self: Never be available on a Friday for questions you can't find the answer to. You will obsess about it all weekend and get no rest from the meat-grinder. Why did it have to ruin my Friday? Why did I let it?

Our team comes in second. Everyone drinks alcohol but me, but afterwards I am so exhausted and emotionally churned out that I actually sleep through the night. The emotions rose like a strong wave all Friday night, then they dissipated as Saturday and Sunday wore on. It feels a little like a hangover. An emotional hangover. Where is the Coca Cola and ibuprofen!?

Dave wants to help me with this hangover. He has been trying desperately to support me in any way he can. He wants to help me "keep my finger on the button." It's something we have said for most of our marriage. The mere presence of an escape button helps people remain in and then push through stressful, painful situations, even if they never use it to escape.

So, he is most happy to force me off the island once a quarter, presumably to a remote tropical place, secluded from all worries and questions without answers. Weren't white sand beaches one of the motivating factors for coming to Southeast Asia? He books a cool little place three hours south of Penang on the western coast of Malaysia for a getaway, and my boss approves it.

Monday, September 19, 2005

I go into a one-on-one with Luke. He asks if I remember his statement in July that pegged his risk of leaving as "high."

"Yes," I say, and the hair on the back of my neck stands at

attention.

"Well, I hope you have a succession plan for me because I am giving my notice. I have a new job in another city. My last day here will be September 30."

I smile and breathe a deep, exhausted, and possibly envious sigh. "Good for you, Luke. I am so happy for you." And it's true. I really am.

But now I have eleven vacancies, and there is a hiring freeze in our department. This means I must go to the top executive for approval to hire anyone to do the work that these people used to do.

When I express my concern to my boss, disguising my terror, and begin to make efforts to learn their jobs, Juliana says, "You are *not* to do their jobs. You will delegate these tasks to someone else."

What? To whom? My people are working 60-70 hours per week. Where will they find the bandwidth to do these tasks?

I immediately go back to my desk to look up Luke's HR records. I click on the "Performance" page and there, on his profile, next to "Risk of Leaving," it says "Low." Regardless of why Juliana left it that way, I am cooked. Luke clearly told us "High," and whatever flag that should have been raised for me and HR was not raised because Juliana optimistically pegged his risk of departure at "Low."

I don't know why it is imperative for me to see that, but I'm furious that it was left that way. I realize, at this moment, I've been set up to fail. I do not for a moment believe it was intentional, but it's happened.

On the way home in Rafeeq's car, the police stop him for a routine insurance check. I sit in the backseat and cry into my black sweater. Rafeeq tries to comfort me and says, "It is okay. They will not do anything to us." I'm not able to explain to him that I am not afraid the police will do something to us. I am just so overwhelmed with everything that needed to be made right.

Oddly, during this time, I keep capturing my thoughts in the lines of country songs or favorite movies, and I don't often listen to country music. I feel original thought evades me, but I can still use others' words to describe what's going on.

In the corner of my mind, I go to Gilley's in Pasadena to sit on a barstool alone with my head hanging down, country music gently strumming in the background. The lyrics to 'Long Haired Country Boy' keep running through my head. Charlie Daniels knew a little something about being criticized.

I have delusions that I'll be destitute, that I've already bankrupted my family. I decide I'll just go live in my brother's basement in West Texas.

Just one problem: he doesn't have a basement. Whatever.

I think to myself, "Poor people have poor ways." I realize I am not a master of the universe and never should have pretended to be one. My secret has been exposed. I'm a nobody and I'm nothing. Throw me away.

What has put me into this tailspin? Thoughts of money, Sean, and my mom.

I don't stop thinking about that clause in my contract that requires me to pay back the amount that it cost Nocura to move me overseas. It's based on months stayed, divided by 12. If I stay for 6 months, I have to pay half of the moving costs. I don't know how much the bill will be, but it could be $15,000 or $50,000. I chastise myself non-stop. Why did I take this risk?

Plus, if I leave, Sean is going to be bounced around from school to school the way I was. I think going to ten different schools was *not* good for me. How could I have done this to my family?

One night, after work, my mom calls to tell me she has a serious condition called polycythemia. She must move down off the mountain in New Mexico because the thin air at high elevations makes the condition worse. Is she going to die before I can get there? Now this weighs on top of all my other guilt, fear, and shame!

It has become even more difficult for me to eat. I exist on Nature Valley granola bars, peanuts, and fried chicken from the Nocura canteen. Those are the only things that even sound good. And I have to wait for a "good moment" in the day so I can choke them down.

I begin to have recurring thoughts of jumping off the 23rd floor balcony. Late at night, the apartment is dark, I'm awake and confused, and I walk around, then lie down on the cold tile floor. The heaviest feeling is guilt. I feel badly that I'm not at home to help my mom with her illness. How do I get out of this mess I've made?

I wonder what they would find if I jumped? Would it be horrible? Or would it be bloodless like a corpse in a sanitized cop show?

The next morning, I ask Dave to begin locking the sliding glass doors before he goes to bed. "Please hide the key for now," I say.

This happens more than once, so when I'm alone at night, I don't go near the balcony or the sliding glass doors leading to it. I'm afraid I'll jump. I feel pathetic and creepy for these thoughts. But they keep coming.

Chapter 9
DON'T BE AFRAID OF ANYBODY

Tuesday, September 20, 2005 - Penang, Malaysia

My brothers, Jim and John, hear that I'm having a difficult time. They are strong men who have always worked hard for what they've gotten. I like to think we're all a lot alike. When I graduated from college, John gave me a birthday card that said, "Here's a bag of crap. (Open card)... That's so you don't have to take any crap from anyone else." He believes, as I do, that if you work hard and assert yourself, anyone can do fine in business.

John writes me two emails that I wish I could say inspired me. Normally I would love and respond to this kind of "buck up" encouragement. Not now, however.

-----Original Message-----
From: John
To: Janna Donovan

Subject: DON'T QUIT
JANNA LYNN, I KNOW IT'S TOUGH, BUT WE WEREN'T RAISED TO BE QUITTERS. YOU CAN DO THIS. DON'T BE AFRAID OF ANYBODY.
JOHN

-----Original Message-----
From: John
To: Janna Donovan
Subject: ON SECOND THOUGHT.
I FORGOT, TELL THEM TO KISS YOUR ASS, YOU'RE TAKING A WEEK OFF, GET YOUR HEAD RIGHT & BARE DOWN!
JOHN

It made me think about the things I have said to people in the past. I now wonder if my words had the opposite effect than I intended. Did I drive them deeper into the hole, rather than motivating them out of it?

Sunday, September 25, 2005

Last night, I woke up every five minutes. Today, I ask some friends to care for Sean so Dave and I can talk. We go to a local café, and I sit down with my little pink notebook with the prison wall hash marks. "Dave, I don't know any other way to say this. Can I quit?" I say it flat, but it comes out like a whine. Then I sing him a Merle Haggard song called "Are the Good Times Really Over?"

"Please do quit before you kill one of us," is his reply. He lets out a deep sigh, and it screams *finally!* "At the very least ask for a job in your old division or a leave of absence." He had been saying it all along, but I hadn't been listening. How often does that happen with the one you love most?

Jerry Clower, American comedian from Mississippi, used to tell a story about a man who climbed a tree after a great big raccoon. He fights with the coon and asks his friend on the ground to shoot it.

The friend fears he may shoot the man. The man tells him to just shoot one of them so they can get it over with.

With my decision loosely made in the dark recesses of my mind, I find out Juliana is scheduled to be in Penang on Monday, along with the head of our division. We've scheduled a one-on-one meeting at 10am. She tells me, "I've got some really big news."

I say, "So do I."

Monday, September 26, 2005

During the one-on-one she says, "You tell me yours first."

I use the notes in my pink booklet to remind me of what to say, because I don't trust my memory. I also don't want Juliana to talk me out of what I'm trying to say, so I quote my notes:

"I do not have the proper equipment right now to do my job. If I were a ski instructor and broke my leg, you would not want me on the slopes. My brain has always been my most trusted asset since I kicked an IQ test's ass in 6th grade. But my brain no longer works.

"At this time, I need to either take a leave of absence or quit. I am as astounded as you and every other executive at my lack of decisiveness and failure to truly lead and contribute. I am very ashamed of what I have not been able to do. I know what I said in my interviews was the truth, but maybe I oversold myself."

She says, "Janna, everyone does that when they're interviewing. We all project our best self. And I hate to tell you this but making the transition to working abroad seems to be more difficult for Americans. I don't know why that is. Now, you are certainly welcome to take some time off, but I'm not convinced that you would get a great deal of rest. You'd just be thinking about what you were coming back to."

She is extremely empathetic. She is tender and kind. She is genuinely concerned. I'm touched and relieved.

Then Juliana tells me she is pregnant with her second child and is due in January. She offers to coach me on priority setting and saying no. She wants to help in any way she can. She wants me to consider my options and be careful about the decisions I am making. I agree to make an action plan to share with her on Wednesday night after the monthly Seminar dinner at 32, a beautiful restaurant that's an expat favorite in Penang.

Wednesday, September 28, 2005

Wednesday night arrives, and I go to 32 with Juliana and Mark Denning. A long, beautiful table is laid before us in a private, candlelit room. Gauze curtains catch the ocean breeze as we begin our first course.

Juliana and I quietly go to a side room with large, overstuffed chairs and I give Juliana the following plan of action. I dutifully list the boxes I'll check each day to ensure I'm being a good girl.

- Tell someone how I'm doing once a week, preferably a director

- Set priorities 3 times a week, Monday-Wednesday-Friday
- Daily exercise
- Keep a list of questions, bother people with them: Ian, Haruto, Liz, Janet
- Take a quarterly trip off the island
- Make a list of accomplishments each day before I go home
- 15 minutes of meditation before I join my family so I can leave work at work
- Fact-based affirmations stated daily
- Learn to meet Cognitive Distortions with Corrective Thoughts

After the dinner, Mark comes out to the garden where Juliana and I are hidden, stands me up and hugs me. He says, "Good God, Janna. Give yourself a break! You've been on the job less than a quarter. You just need to use what you learned in the US. You know what to do." He seems like a good father. Strong, forceful, positive, concerned, and wanting me to be confident.

I am not looking forward to telling Dave how I let Juliana talk me into staying. I don't even know how it happened myself.

Thursday, September 29 – Friday, September 30, 2005

The following day, my notes from Juliana's coaching session on setting business priorities become a jumble. One half are secret, personal information and the other half are unintelligible business-speak:

South Asia sales, better monitoring, cost-effective placement, make team accountable, what has to happen for this Marketing

System to work? Give them a framework, a management system. Make sure it has the data, function, process. Protect the team. Manage upward. Make the VP successful. Explain the sales issues. Push back. Next week: Learn the new model. How do we work together? They have to fix it, not me. What do they need? Know your critical few. Learn to be a leader. Think about one thing you'd like to achieve, not just 400 emails. Don't get distracted.

But in the margin, I write:

Prolonged anxiety attacks, needing to tell someone each week, unable to be around my family without feeling agitated, depressed, self-centered, unable to leave work at work, hiding in the bathroom…

And just like that, the thoughts of jumping off that 23rd floor balcony return.

Never before, have I allowed my inbox to grow so large. Everyone copies everyone here, even just to say "thanks." Oy.

I used to manage my priorities and tasks by what was looming in my inbox, but I've quickly learned that upper-level managers cannot afford to do that. I create separate inboxes and move 1,000 emails at a time over to those boxes. I make room for more crucially important news that is sure to come my way each day.

My general manager, Liz, sees me at a birthday party when I have my guard down. She asks if I'm okay and can tell by my silence that I am not. She gives me a book called *Feel the Fear and Do It Anyway* by Susan Jeffers. When I get home, I earnestly try to complete the exercises that the book recommends. I begin to write life goals and create affirmations and write them down on cards and carry them with me.

I never thought I would be like the character parodied on *Saturday Night Live* telling himself he's good and smart and likeable. But here I am, doing it and saying it to myself. At this point, I'll try anything to not go stark, raving mad.

I think you're supposed to only have three, but I grind away at affirmations too.

I am loved, I am strong, I am a fighter, I am smart, I am funny, I ask for help, I stay in touch with loved ones, I take care of my body, I am responsible. If I don't know, I find the answer. There is time to find the answer if I don't know, I make good decisions, I am forgiven, I am not a victim, I can think, I relax after work, I relax on the weekends, I keep moving on the weekends, I make a home for myself on the weekends, I do the best I can, I work hard, I ask the *team* for the data, I am positive and encouraging, I am sincere, I focus on now, I can make it.

But my affirmations are so far from reality. I have zero time with my family except on weekends. I never even get home in time to kiss my son goodnight.

I don't even know him right now.

Several of my worst days at Nocura involve getting a call from the headmaster telling me that Sean has been naughty in some way. Don't they have Dave's phone number?! He pronounces 'water' now with a hard T, like a Brit, not an American. He asks, "Have I been there before?" and when he says "been" it sounds like the legume, not the nickname for a guy named Benjamin.

But the saddest comment from him comes during the worst of my depression, and I feel so guilty.

"I don't want to be in this family," he says with desperation in his voice.

Saturday, October 1 – Sunday, October 2, 2005
Pulau Pangkor

We go on our planned vacation to Pulau Pangkor for some rest, and it couldn't come sooner. We ride in a freezing bus for three hours, but we arrive to warmth and sand and water. It's pristine and beautiful. We stay at a little inn that is rustic and run by nice people.

As we hike to the beach, I notice that Dave is wearing an old, worn-out Nocura T-shirt from a sales event three years prior. I look at him and say, "Really? You had to choose that shirt? I can't even come to a remote island without seeing that name?!"

All this time, Dave has been asking me to get angry, to tell others that they have played a part in the mess I'm in. It seems the only anger I am able to feel is directed inwardly, never outwardly.

"You became a less confident businessperson when you went back to thinking about spiritual things and seeking God," Dave says to me. "People who aren't into that seem more sure and less worried about making one little mistake!"

I inwardly agree with a little envy in my heart, and say, "Yeah, how do they have more faith than those of us who supposedly have faith in God?"

In Pulau Pangkor, something very small but powerful happens while I am lying awake on yet another sleepless

night, counting the hundreds of geckos on the wall.
I begin to fight back.
I answer the negative voices with a gusto that comes from somewhere I can't name.

"You're immature."
"I paid for two houses."

"You have become a crisis-maker."
"I work it out."

"I'm the only one to blame."
"Everyone makes mistakes."

"I'll die because of this."
"Plenty of people take meds, get better, and get on with their lives."

"I'm repelling people instead of attracting them."
"When I'm on, I'm still funny and happy."

"I'm avoiding responsibility."
"I've been accountable in admitting my problems."

"If I leave, I will be giving Sean the kind of childhood I had, moving every two years."
"He will learn to cope."

"Details escape me, never clear."
"I have always researched thousands of details."

"I'm lazy."
"I've worked since I was 15, long hours, then did chores at home."

"I'm broken."
"I forgive you."

"I'm tired."
"I'm trying to get you some rest."

On the way home from Pulau Pangkor, I begin to ask a difficult question:

Would it be okay morally if I left Nocura? Would God be ashamed of me if I quit?

Exhaustion. Understaffed. 40% of positions not filled. Pushing people harder with little to no support. It is all so confused and fast paced, and no one is letting us off the hook because of this.

Monday, October 3, 2005

My problem feels like a spiritual conundrum, so I desperately set up a meeting with my new pastor, Craig. Dave comes with me to the Starbucks, but I've told Craig the wrong Starbucks. He walks 40 minutes in the pouring rain, because his wife has the SUV. We finally meet up, and I am so apologetic and grateful all at the same time.

I tell Craig that I feel I have made a huge mistake in demanding that my family come here; that my arrogance drove me to demand that we move. I explain that I thought it would be good for my husband's spiritual journey, and I immediately realize how religious, pious, and controlling that sounds. And, by the way, Craig, can I have some immediate, actionable feedback? I have to leave for a conference call with Nocura executives in 30 minutes.

He laughs. "Speed counseling? I love it," he says under his breath and dives in.

Craig explains how he sees my situation unfolding. He shares three major ideas. One, to call oneself "depressed" is to step into a label which, in many ways, can block change. Two, he tells me I have all these thoughts like extra weights that I carry around as I try to make decisions or think clearly. I'm trying to be a Supermom, fulfill my desire to live overseas, and direct the spiritual life of my husband, all the while feeling guilty for things out of my control and worrying needlessly about failure, competency, friends, and doubt. He draws a stick figure with huge platters held high in the air. I can't possibly be agile or decisive with all these "big ideas" weighing in each time I take a breath.

"What do you like to do?" he asks.

"Hmmm. Nothing anymore."

"Well, when you used to like to do stuff, what did you like to do?"

"Wayyyy back when I used to like to do things, what did I like to do?" Hmmmm. Think. I try to give him an answer, but there is no excitement behind any of them. When I'm depressed like this, I'm absolutely no fun to help.

As painful for him as it was for me, we conclude our talk. He writes me a prescription:

"I give you permission to be kind to yourself every day. Meditate, get a massage, go to funny movies, laugh, go to (but don't host) a party, exercise or run. Write down the thoughts that assail you. Then, just next to them, write down the indisputable truth that combats that thought. Concentrate on the truth side of the page."

'Great,' I think to myself, cracking a smile. 'I got a head start on this with the geckos on Pulau Pangkor.

His final words to me are, "It's more important what God does in you than what He does through you." I consider all of this excellent advice from a man who has seen God fix a lot of people's mistakes. I do feel better.

Of course, that doesn't last. I attend the conference call on my mobile phone while in a cab on the way to work. I get on the second conference call of the day and hear executives discussing a decision that I can't believe they're going to make.

They want to switch to a *new* advertising agency for all ads placed in South Asia. It will save us tens of thousands annually. Sounds good on the surface, doesn't it?

It's not.

I can't believe it. That little cost savings cannot possibly be more important than the chaos that is about to ensue. Confusion will escalate by 1000 percent. People from other teams are filling in for my advertising team, and any new recruits for the positions will be clueless how Nocura does business. Who is supposed to teach the new agency about the details of how we want things to be done? I already know the answer.

Me.

I guess that job will fall to me. I stammer out a plea for us to wait a month before implementing the decision. "Yes," comes the answer. "We'll wait a month."

Then I remember Luke is gone. 'Oh God, help me to not

jump off one of the balconies tonight.'

I'm back to feeling scared and guilty. It's as if an enemy has me right where he wants me. Why do I continue? Do I want an expat lifestyle? Is it worth it? My team...they all know how to survive. Why don't I?

I have trouble setting aside the time to attend Sean's parent-teacher conference. That's a cliché that only happens in the movies, right? The screenwriter bludgeons you with the fact that the protagonist is putting work ahead of his family. Then the spouse gets upset when the protagonist cannot even take a tiny amount of time off to do something necessary for their child.

The sick irony is that I am putting a job I *hate* ahead of my family's needs. That is the one fact of which I am most ashamed. It's like an addiction. I wasn't raised this way.

Or was I?

Chapter 10
GAMES PEOPLE PLAY

Tuesday, October 4, 2005 - Penang, Malaysia

It's Tuesday and time for a one-on-one with a team member, Ismail, to talk about his career path at Nocura. We go to a conference room. I catch a glimpse of Haruto Ideka, the exec who first tried to hire me to Asia. He goes into an adjacent conference room with one of the strongest leaders from my team, Marion.

Back to Ismail. I love career planning with people who report to me. It opens up all kinds of possibilities for them and motivates them to perform well in their current role as they prepare for the next stage. I tell them to take the bull by the horns and own the process as everyone must do at Nocura. But this one is very difficult for me.

Ismail's performance has been solid. He's doubled the amount of vendor participation money we receive each quarter. He's done what's been asked of him, and I really like Ismail personally. He is sincere, ethical, and motivated, and in our discussion, he explains what move he thinks will be best for him and his family.

But I feel ridiculous. While he talks, I cannot concentrate on any of his words. He asks me if his position will change with the upcoming reorganization. Will his boss change?

I don't know what to say and I do a terrible job of being vague, because that's what was asked of me. Is this what it's like playing the game of life on drugs?

After an hour, the meeting mercifully ends. My disappointment at not being able to lead Ismail gives me a dull, sickening pain in my stomach. Why have I failed him? Why am I failing everybody?

When I'm finished with the one-on-one, Haruto comes by my cube and says, "Hey, when were you planning on going home today?" I tell him six and he says, "My driver and I will take you." It sounds ominously perky and perkily ominous.

At 6:05pm I climb into Haruto's van. Both of us take a seat in the second row behind his driver. I feel like I've been kidnapped by Haruto as the van door slides shut. He asks me how it's going and how my team is. I am as candid with him as I have ever been with anyone since arriving in Southeast Asia. I trust him and have from the moment I landed in Malaysia.

"Haruto, something terrible has happened to me. I feel foolish telling you in such dramatic terms, but I cannot think any more. I cannot lead my team as they deserve to be led."

Halfway through the drive, Haruto, in his charming, aggressive way, says, "Janna, why don't you quit? What is stopping you?"

"Because, in the future, what if Sean wants to quit sports or something else just because he doesn't like it? What will I tell him? I want to be able to look him in the face and say,

'Press on, persevere' because it's the right thing to do."

"You know what, Janna?" continues Haruto. "You don't have to tell him anything. Or tell him that his mother is needed back in the US for another project. You are well respected there. No one back there cares what you did in Asia. They won't even know. Forget Nocura! It is not worth what you're going through. You were sent here with one set of skills, and you were asked to use them in a totally different company."

I could have kissed him.

Wednesday, October 5, 2005

I go for my one-on-one with Liz, my general manager. She asks how it's going, and I say, "Here's where we're at with demand. With me and my ability to make decisions? Still not going well."

She says, "I know what you're going through, Janna. I have been there during some rough times in my life. Your strength is difficult to get back. I totally sympathize." We're both quiet for a moment. Then she says, "But, in the end, that is my personal reaction. Personal is personal and business is business. If things don't improve soon, I am going to have to make a change."

Not until I'm riding home in the back of Rafeeq's car do I think that Liz and Haruto might have agreed to speak to me and give me the same message.

Are they trying to get me to quit just so I'll have to pay back the relocation cost?

No. What a paranoid thought about two people who are delivering the right answer. They are not villains, even if I'm a bit naïve. We are *not* in a Hollywood movie. I have never known someone to conspire to "do me in," and that is not what's happening here.

My head seems very clear after talking to Haruto and Liz. They say I am lucky because I have options. We have money from our house sale. I have Dave and Sean. I can take a rest. I can give everyone a rest from worrying about me. They are telling me what I want to hear. They are telling me I can go home.

But quitting is not what I came here to do. I have begged God for this chance like a child begs for his first bike. I have wanted to live and work abroad since I can remember.

When I was a child, we had a set of burgundy, leatherbound encyclopedias. All around the inside covers there were tiny drawings of children from around the world. I always dreamed of going to where those children were. I wanted to see the little Dutch girls' wooden shoes and the Mexican boys' maracas and the Chinese boys' pointed hats.

Shortly after Dave and I married, we made a plan to save our money, quit our jobs, then travel around the world. And we did it! We travelled for four years and fantasized about living in each place we visited. We talked a lot about moving to Costa Rica, Mexico, or any place tropical where we could make a living. But talk was all we did.

I've finally done more than just visit, and now it has turned out so differently than I expected. I did not come here to embarrass myself or my family. But I feel that's all I've done. I've come here to succeed, to prove to myself that I can be an open, compassionate manager *and* be successful. In this I've failed.

On Thursday, Haruto calls a special meeting. Myself, all

the leaders on my team, as well as several senior managers throughout CAC are present. This is odd because none of us are in Haruto's organization. When we arrive in the conference room, several executives from Tokyo, including my boss, Juliana, are also in the meeting via speakerphone. I look around the table and realize Marion is already in the conference room. I don't go to my usual director spot. I go to the end of the table in a quiet, humble, I'm-about-to-get-fired way of walking.

Haruto begins what feels like a negative, yet sincere focus group. "We are going through a difficult time in Nocura right now. We want to get your thoughts about what morale is like in your teams, what you think needs to change, and how we can help."

No one talks. Haruto is forced to go around the table and ask us all individually. "Chong, what are you thinking?"

"I am braindead. Let someone else answer." After five months of working seven days a week, it is the most positive response they should expect from Chong, a long-term veteran.

Marion speaks up and says she is resentful of last-minute decisions that continue to keep her team here until 9:00pm, only to be changed the following morning. She cannot be asked to improve employee survey scores when this happens every week. It dawns on me that she must have gone to Haruto last week when I placed the final straw on the camel's back.

The charismatic manager of a high-end components team, Andy, had desperately wanted to run a promotion for the last month of the quarter. He had been seriously missing his numbers and needed the website to reflect the new prices immediately. He emailed everyone several requests for the last-minute change, and they'd said no. So, he came to my desk and asked me. With a shrug, I stopped the string of objecting emails by typing, "Yes, whatever Andy needs." Marion's team had to stay late once again. They felt betrayed by me.

Despite coming in with the best intentions, the work-life balance of my employees has actually worsened during my tenure.

The executives begin to talk more, putting words into our mouths. Juliana and Haruto are more empathetic, encouraging, and reasonable, in touch with what we are feeling, even if we won't say it out loud.

Finally, Brandon, a manager fresh from the US, gets forceful. He says, "Okay, you all need to be leaders. You need to be positive and stop all this negative thinking. Whatever you need to do this weekend, have a few beers, kick the dog, whatever. But I want you all to come in next Monday with a smile on your face, ready to go at this last month of the quarter. We will *not* miss our numbers this quarter."

I sit there listening to Brandon and think of a scene in *Silverado* in which Mal (played by Danny Glover) has just risked his life to protect a box of gold from the bad guys, only to be accused of wanting it for himself. He says, "Mister, you got a lot to learn about people."

Brandon doesn't know how hard they've been working, how poorly they've been led by me, how they've been giving everything they have in a very difficult market where our sales and our margins are under more pressure than Nocura will admit.

Leaders, to their credit, have been quick to set goals for

increasing my engagement. They have been right in some of their attempts. I did not need more vacation, more perks, or higher pay. What do I want? Mostly the same things most of us want (confirmed in the book *First Break All the Rules* by Buckingham and Coffman):

- Tell me each week something I did right. Recognize the good.
- Be clear about what you expect out of me. Be clear about the priorities each week.
- Ensure that I have what I need, including training, time, and staff.
- Make sure I'm well suited for the position I'm in, that it's playing to my strengths.
- Make sure someone cares about my improvement, and my development. My job is something they can take away from me, but they can't take away what I've learned.

My multiple bosses are open-minded, ethical, curious people. They've tried to give me what I want, and in return, I've tried to not whine to their face. But then it all got so chaotic.

I did not want to play games, but I know I started to. I did not want to do less while my division was missing its goals and so many people were struggling with motivation. I asked leaders to be clearer about priorities. I asked for better decisions when they didn't acknowledge the part they were playing in our misses. I thought I gave them what they asked for. But I feel like nothing I did made a difference.

After the meeting, a plan begins to circulate among execs. I receive an email that explains the re-organization. I am demoted to just running the advertising placement for

Singapore (two levels below what I was hired to do).

I thought I'd feel relieved, but I feel nauseated and stunned to finally see the change.

Tuesday, October 11, 2005.

Last Thursday I started my new position in advertising. I think they figured if I cannot handle the big picture, perhaps detail will help me grasp what I need to grasp.

Juliana notifies the larger team of the rearrangement of responsibilities. I want so badly to explain to people, "This isn't the real me. I wish you knew me when I was stronger. I would have led you out of this mess."

But Juliana has already warned me about saving face with Asians. She says they will find my display of weakness repulsive. "They need you to play the game," she says. "They'd rather not know. Play the game."

In an odd way, I do feel a little relief. I am no longer the person everyone goes to for decisions. Now I can just be an individual contributor.

A little rebellious streak raises its head. Dave and I begin to exchange smart alec emails and it feels good to laugh. Movie lines continue to be a favorite way for Dave and me to communicate. It's like a secret code, especially if you watch obscure movies that your teammates aren't old enough to remember: *Say Anything*, *Office Space*, and Dave's favorite, filmed in our hometown, *Slacker*.

But, in between our movie references, Dave shows me a story he read in Stephen Ambrose's 1997 *Citizen Soldiers*—a book about US Army soldiers moving inland from the Normandy beaches and through Europe until Germany's surrender. I don't think he means to depress me further, but he does. He tells me:

"A former World War II colonel talks about how the soldiers with the best performance during training and the loudest promises to kill the enemy are the ones that fold when they enter combat. They turn tail and run away from the front, never to be heard from again."

I feel sick to my stomach. My mind thinks, 'I can see that. Those who like the structure, challenge, and clarity of training do well. Then they get into the fray of battle and cannot deal with the chaos, the ambiguity, the gray.' Then my heart says, 'I never wanted to be one of those people, but now I am.'

Even with reduced responsibility, my body is not holding up well under the pressure. My teeth and gums hurt for some strange reason. The moist flesh of my gums and around my eyes is white because of anemia. My breath, urine and skin have a very unpleasant smell. My toenails are coming off one by one. My face has the look of someone who's just witnessed the Holocaust. I have a permanent worried frown with deep, angry creases between my eyes, but I'm not angry.

Many people are now discussing me and my situation when I am not around. Dave speaks regularly with Dan, his brother-in-law, who is a lifeline for my struggling husband. Mom makes her daily call to Dave to ask what he's done about bringing me home. My brothers, Jim and John, have spoken to my father. I think they've used the phrase "nervous breakdown." Wow, how 70s.

Colleagues at work say that I don't look like the same

person who arrived in July. They comment on how much weight I've lost or ask, "That's all you're going to eat?" no matter what I bring back from the Nocura canteen. They leave little gifts of food at my desk or pretend to not be able to finish something they know I love. Even Janet, Liz's administrative assistant, orders me fish and chips whenever there's an exec lunch. For people who want me to pretend as if nothing is wrong, they certainly seem kind and concerned and very aware that I am not playing the game.

Different people email me prescriptions and advice. Some of it is crucial to my very survival. Other messages are very condescending, and I am offended. In my state, I conclude that if you don't like people talking about you behind your back or giving you trite advice, you better not get messed up. Don't get cancer, don't have a miscarriage, and definitely do *not* get depressed. Don't allow yourself to fall into a state of weakness.

I begin to have the thought, 'You can just go to the airport. You have a gold card in your wallet. Walk into the terminal, buy a ticket to Houston, and fly away, Janna!' I'm sure I would do it if I thought I could fly for 30 hours, stuck in a metal tube, without a panic attack. Visions of federal marshals taking me off the plane after a freak out abruptly end the thoughts of escape.

I begin to think back to all the people I've known who have struggled with depression and exhaustion. I don't really know the details of what they went through during their private difficulty, but I begin to piece together certain facts, and their moods and actions make more and more sense. These ghosts of my past weren't weak or lazy; they were exhausted and depressed.

My uncle Bill returned from Vietnam and sat staring out into the garden for a year. My best friend's mother had finally told off her very meticulous, wealthy husband and we began seeing her in her pajamas every day. A generous man we knew just ended it all one day at a river bridge. My great uncle cried a lot after falling into a vat of chemicals meant for cattle, then ended his life early. My brilliant next-door neighbor in grad school had her black and white sock days.

Wednesday morning, I make myself choke down some cereal. I've lost 30 pounds, from 133 to 103.

Chapter 11
THE BIG DAY

Friday, October 14, 2005 - Penang, Malaysia

On Thursday night, I skip the team dinner with Juliana and come home at a decent time. I spend several relaxed hours with Dave just talking about whether I'm ready to quit or not, and how good it would be to make a final decision. Can I really do it? I'm the only one who knows.

The following day, Friday, I meet with Juliana first thing. I still don't know how I am going to tell her. We talk about how her pregnancy is going and how she is feeling. I try to have some social skills but come across flat and faded, obviously trying very hard. She says something under her breath about maybe not wanting to do this to people.

She asks, "Well, what do you want to do?"

"Today, or for the rest of my life?" A weak attempt at humor. I can't be distracted from what I must do.

"Well, I need to go. I need to leave Nocura. I'm exhausted and my body is ceasing to work."

Ahh. Self-preservation finally kicks in.

It. Was. That. *Easy.*

Juliana smiles. I smile back. She immediately talks about the details and how it will be announced. Then I am a little mortified and angry with the next bit of news.

I am not allowed to tell anyone until one week before I walk out the door. No one on my team and no colleague can hear it from me.

She says she knows I will find success in the future and will learn from this, then advises me to not let it defeat me. As soon as the meeting finishes, I go out into the sunshine and call Dave on my cell phone. Thoughts flood my mind. I feel like singing to myself, so like Colonel Pickering in *My Fair Lady*, I say, "I did it! I did it! Really I did it!"

Saturday, October 15, 2005

Oktoberfest has been planned at the German-Malaysian Society's grounds. I've been waiting for this party since I came for my look-see interview with Nocura. Dave and I, Liz, and some other friends decide to go together. No more thinking about shipments and flights back home for Dave and me. We get to just enjoy the moment while it feels good.

The food smells and tastes great. Sausages, potatoes, beer. An old-fashioned band plays. Sean runs around with friends from school. It feels like we're back in New Braunfels, Texas, at Würstfest, only we're dressed for a warm evening in Penang. Haruto arrives with his family and others from their luxury high-rise apartment building. The young party crowd has turned out and they invite us to sit with them.

We are feelin' groovy. So groovy that when Mike, an American who's been here for seven years, asks me to polka,

I say yes, and we immediately head to the dance floor. Mike's from New York and I'm from Texas. Our Polish, Czech, and German grandparents would have been proud that he and I know how to polka. Apparently, we are some of the only ones in Penang who do. He spins and spins and spins me for at least three songs. I am getting dizzy but am grinning from ear to ear. We come off the dance floor laughing and smiling. At the edge, looking at me from his seat, is Haruto, clapping and smiling.

And the thoughts begin. This is fun. These people are fun. This is why expats get out and party. Why did I quit? I could have made it. I don't want to miss this next year. Maybe I can tell them on Monday that I'm fine, never mind. I'll go on the anti-depressants, get the chemicals straight in my brain. Beat this.

Dave sees the wheels start to turn and says, "Don't even think about it." Too late.

Still, that night I go home to try anti-depressants for the first time. I don't sleep at all, and my body twitches the whole night.

Sunday, October 16, 2005

The thoughts begin again, like demons visiting me when I'm at my weakest.

I realize that I have to continue working at Nocura for the next month. I also know I'm about to be asked to fire people. Not the way I imagined my last month.

And then I think, 'Oh, why did I have to dance!?' This is a small town, and everyone saw me on the dance floor with Mike. They surely all think I'm faking my physical exhaustion.

I can hear them saying, sarcastically, "She's not at full capacity? Riiiiight." I feel I've made Haruto look like a fool. He originally recruited me to the region, and he's gone to bat for me. He's given me credibility and understanding advice when I needed it most.

But what they don't understand is when I see a break in the clouds, no matter how brief, I take every opportunity to get out and act normal. I write a card to someone. I go make a small purchase I've been putting off for four weeks. I quickly do all I can, because I know the window is going to shut again and I'll be left helpless, unable to leave the quicksand by my own power or choosing.

How do I believe all is lost? Where is my hope? Why do I not care if I win or lose? When did I last care if I won or lost?

When I was interviewing for this job.

It's my name. It's Sean's name. Donovan. I've tarnished it. I got overwhelmed. I couldn't fight back. I feel more isolated from Sean and Dave than ever.

I thought the pretending at work would be over now that I've given my notice. But I still have to fake it until I walk out of here for good.

I chose to give proper notice, but it is very hard to work and live in this "limbo" state here at the end. I could have chosen to quit with no notice, but that would have been very hard for me to do. Not being able to tell my co-workers I'm leaving makes my skin crawl. It's like knowing that you're getting a divorce but still living with your family through the December holidays. It's always at the back of your mind.

I need to sleep but I let the fear overcome me instead. The guilt, the shame. Sometimes I can stop and just relax and say, "Ahhhhhh, I did it. I finally said no to Nocura." But it's still not enough to get some sleep. Not enough to lighten up.

I must answer emails. Can't with my brain fried. Supposed to be relaxing, kicking back. But what's light and breezy right now? What's good? What will make me and others smile? Weather's warm and sunny, and my family loves me. At least I think they still do.

Got to learn to love me. How do I reconcile myself to that? How do I train myself to that? How do I train others on how to treat me? I told Nocura, "Enough," but I turned it around and made it all my fault. I guess I wasn't the person big enough to come in and fix the problems. I took an action. I quit. Now I find fault with myself because of this decision too?

I feel so separated from Sean over this. *Why...?* Because Sean has little regard for me, so little need for me. *Wow.*

He is one of the few reasons I haven't killed myself. If I keep thinking he doesn't need me, then what will become of me?

STOP!

Got to fight back. Got to fight for myself. Got to think of someone and something else outside myself.

How dare I not believe God loves me? I have so much when others have so little. Dave, Sean, my health, Tara, my parents, love, eyes that see.

In fact, the big, fat irony is that we have more money at this time in our life than we've ever had. The sale of the house and the increase in our investments means that our net worth climbed higher than pre-September 11 levels. I am here with material wealth that allows me so many choices, but I can't make any. I have so much, but the ability to enjoy it is locked somewhere deep within me. God, please help me find the key.

Dave sees me struggle. He encourages me daily by

reminding me of the hard times we've survived together. More importantly, he reminds me of the forgiveness we've already given one another.

-----Original Message-----
From: David Donovan
To: Janna Donovan
Subject: Forgiveness
Janna
Forgiveness is a choice. Feelings take time after the choice is made...as cited in "wild at heart". You must forgive yourself. Once you make that choice...to turn off the flame, the water will stop boiling and will begin to cool. Take this as book from a man who has forgiven both you and himself. First comes the choice of forgiveness, then it will take time for the feelings to soften.
Jumpa lagi DaveD

-----Original Message-----
From: Janna Donovan
To: David Donovan
Subject: RE: Forgiveness
I must forgive myself, yes. How do I let go? I must turn off the boiling water. I want to. The water boils more at work but somehow I feel relief afterward.
Janna

Thursday, October 20, 2005

Nocura lets me know how much my claw back will cost. Dave cannot believe that I am so willing to pay it back after the wholesale changes they made to the job I was hired for.

But the total is RM25,556, which equals almost $10,000. SO worth it!

But why did I promise Juliana I'd continue for six weeks? What's the point?

I quit so I could get some relief, but now I'm working hurt with the knowledge that I am about to be gone. I don't want to sit in meetings six weeks from now and be asked why I made this or that decision. I don't want to make decisions because, right now, I'm an idiot. I desperately wish I could just get off this merry-go-round.

Liz continues to include me socially and invite our family over, even though I am surely a pariah at work. She's planning a Halloween party.

-----Original Message-----
From: Janna Donovan
To: David Donovan
Subject: Liz wants to include us
Liz is amazing, she can be frustrated with me over work but accept me as I am and wants to do lots of things with our family outside of work.
She and you and everyone amaze me.
Janna

-----Original Message-----
From: David Donovan
To: Janna Donovan
Subject: RE: Liz wants to include us
I don't know why you have to take this journey, but you need to learn how to accept the love that is given you without looking for a

reason why it shouldn't be given, why you don't deserve it. Sorry if I'm being a little heavy during work time. See you soon. I love you.
Dave

As the days roll along, Dave ceases to hide his impatience with me and his disdain for how I've handled this entire situation. I don't think he can comprehend how afraid I am of being left for dead. At this time in my life, I cannot support myself financially. That feels weird. I feel like an old woman that people are caring for and planning to put away.

Just as bad, the relationship between Mom and Dave has escalated into vehement fighting about what should be happening in my life, so I give my mother Tara's contact information. I think I'm getting Tara involved to give some sanity to the conversations. I don't want Dave and my mom to be the only ones with decision-making power. Tara is a professional psychologist with 20 years' experience. Is this too much to ask of my longest running friendship?

We talk on the phone. Tara is concerned about me only sleeping one hour a night, week after week. She says it can make me suicidal and has made people homicidal. She's not sure about losing my toenails. "Ewww," we both laugh. After I describe an obsession with showering, she explains that I may need an illusion of control. I can't get the smell off my skin. Am I dying?

Dave is becoming so tired of my up and down life. He is frustrated because, no matter how he tries to help, I complain that it's not what I need. I am annoying as all get out, but I can't help myself.

Though, I admit I am frightened when he gets angry. Not because I think he will physically harm me, but because I am so vulnerable. It's as if people being there for me is the only thing left holding my body together. When Dave is angry with me, I just go all limp and search for a place to fall down.

But, occasionally, some truly life-threatening event will come into my consciousness and remind me that, while I may be in trouble, I'm probably not going to die. I feel privately ashamed that I am wasting peoples' prayers and worry on my imaginary illness when there are others who really need their prayers. One such email arrives from a good friend, Benjamin, who writes us to let us know about a mutual friend who has been living with cancer for several years.

-----Original Message-----
From: Benjamin
To: David Donovan
Subject: RE: Happy Birthday

Dave,
I called Zach in New York yesterday. He was out but I had a chance to talk to Isabella. She was very frank and open about the course of his brain cancer. The news has not been good lately. Even after the surgery and after over two months of convalescence, the cancer has returned.
Zach goes to the doctor every two days. It is not good and if his general health does not improve quickly he will not be able to take another round of chemo. My sense of things, and no drama here Dave, is that there is a fairly good chance Zach may not make it through the year.
Got to go. Tell Janna and Mr. Sean hi.

Friday, October 21, 2005

I still have to go to Daily Product Meetings. Every morning, my team members and I must answer questions from Sales, Branding, and the Product Group about the previous day's demand generation. But we don't have answers. We don't have the time or the resources to find the answers. That doesn't change as time goes by, but they continue to ask us for them every single morning at 11:30. I guess I'd rather look stupid than lie. But it is definitely hard on the ego.

On top of that, I can't stop being addicted to this job I can't do. Some people do what they love, like movie directors, and some have a different calling, like doctors. These people spend inordinate amounts of time away from their families. But their heartfelt love for their job helps their absence from home make sense.

Not me. I hate this job and yet, right now, the *only* time I feel calm is when I'm at Nocura. That is sick. Do I have some sort of weird condition?

Dave reads to me about Vietnam War veterans who say they would go away on RnR (rest and relaxation) but worry the entire time about the devastation waiting for them when they returned. They only felt better when they went back to face it, regardless of how impossible the situation was. It is melodramatic, or even presumptuous of me, to compare myself to a Vietnam veteran, but this nails the feeling on the head.

Being this thin makes a bathtub painful. There's no cushion on my butt bones where there used to be plenty of junk in the trunk. I wonder how Hollywood stars take a bath.

Another irony? I'm skinnier than I've ever been, but I have

no drive to get new clothes and enjoy it. When I muster the courage to shop, I go in the changing room and pull my shorts off without even unzipping them.

Dave and I have a serious discussion about the future. He tells me he wants to stay here a while and not let this place kick our butts.

God, I don't want to let it kick our butts, but how can I stay when it makes me so sad? I wake up startled every morning and say, "Oh, I'm still in this nightmare. It's not over." At times like this, the balcony still seems like a solution.

There are moments of reprieve. I watch an American movie or football game and I lose myself in enjoyment. Then, when the movie is over, I walk outside into the heat, eat food I can't pronounce, dodge the crazy driving, and I remember I still live in Malaysia, 15,000 miles from home.

I write Dave an email with a subject line that I know will get his attention.

-----Original Message-----
From: Janna Donovan
To: David Donovan
Subject: Birthday sex
Besides that, what would you like next Monday?
Janna

-----Original Message-----
From: David Donovan
To: Janna Donovan
Subject: RE: Birthday sex
tom yam at cafe 26?
Dave

I arrange a massage at our apartment for Dave's birthday.

-----Original Message-----
From: David Donovan
To: Janna Donovan
Subject: RE: Hope you're doing well on your birthday
I am doing well on my birthday. The massage was nice. Thanks for setting it up. She really worked my shoulders, and man I never knew my feet were so sore.
Talked with the houston donovans, told them you had quit your job etc. Hope you're having a good day.
Dave

We feel so close at times when we can put away all the pain. Dave is actually shocked to know that I think we're endlessly fighting. Given the circumstances, I have to admit, we are sticking by one another's side as well as any expat couple could expect. I had no idea, when I accepted this position, how many expat marriages end in divorce. It's way above the average for couples who don't go abroad. That's a scary thought.

The rollercoaster nature of work astounds even me. I have quit. I have said, "Uncle." I am ready to move on with my life. Let's wrap things up here and get some rest. Everything is going up from this point on, right? Right?

But every day I wake up and remember that my nightmare is not over. I must get up at 6:00am, shower, ride to work, and sit in a fluorescent, cold prison for 10 hours. My decision to quit does not put the downward slide on hold like I thought it would.

Friday, October 28, 2005

A weeklong vacation is coming soon, so I send Dr. Chang an email. I want to be mentally fit so my family and I can enjoy ourselves, even if it's just for a week. I want to feel like I belong again.

-----Original Message-----
From: Janna Donovan
To: Dr. Chang
Subject: Hello
Hello Dr. Chang,
I feel I am spiraling down to a place that I can't get back from.
I resigned from Nocura but have agreed to keep working here for another month for financial and other reasons.
My husband is growing weary of pulling me up and my son is having difficulty behaving in school.
I don't want to take the medication, but I'm desperate.
I've lost who I was over this. I fear I'm about to lose my husband and son. Will the medication help?
Janna

Dr. Chang emails me back that afternoon.

-----Original Message-----
From: Dr. Chang
To: Janna Donovan
Subject: RE: Hello
Please give the medication a try for at least 1 to 2 months. Discuss with your husband and come up with contingency plans or safety

plans for your fears. If you don't see even a slight improvement by then, you know you have given this particular medication a fair try and it's not for you. That does not mean medications in general won't help. It just means you haven't found your fit.

In the meantime, try to practice some of the things we talked about: positive self-affirmation (just choose 2 powerful ones for you for now), self-care (meaning stop trying to take care of everybody and focus on yourself-it's OK to be "selfish" intentionally once in a while) and practice the mental health hygiene we talked about - 1) Rest 2) Nutrition 3) Exercise 4) Socialise to the best that you can for now (remember the key is "can" NOT "should").

So, if you can only exercise by walking for 10 minutes now, that's GOOD ENOUGH for now!

Please keep me informed of how you are doing, via email or phone. Feel free to contact me when you have questions, doubts, or just want to vent. Same for your husband.

Take care.

Dr. Chang

At work, I'm still skulking around as if I have committed a crime of enormous proportion. I avoid people I know; even hide from people I don't know. I treat situations as if I'm running from the law. This would all be more plausible if I had killed someone or committed some other horrible crime. This is not *Thelma and Louise!*

As I have in previous months, I treat my gold card as my release button. Its mere presence helps me remain in this painful situation, even if I never use it to escape.

If I decide to escape all the chaos and dark thoughts, once and for all, I will walk out of the Nocura complex, take a taxicab or driver to the airport terminal, then I'll buy an

American Airlines ticket for LA. Why does it have to be American Airlines? I don't know. But right now, flying away in a silver American Airlines jet is my most comforting escape fantasy.

Where is the relief? The mental break I so desperately wanted? How in the world can a person go from being okay to seriously thinking about ending it all? I think again about the depressed ghosts I've known from the past that travel with me everywhere now. Their pain seemed to be caused by some unseen force, not a broken leg or a disease. Just an invisible ache that inflicts the heart, and then renders the brain devoid of function and logic.

Triggers for depressing thoughts are everywhere. I can't watch a movie or read a murder mystery or even the Bible without feeling overwhelmed, frightened, or angry at myself.

Earlier in the week, Dave and Dr. Chang talked about my addiction to a job I hate. They even spoke about my illogical demand that all triggers (books, movies, etc.) be removed from our house. She gave Dave the green light to treat me like an addict. It is my responsibility to walk out of this. No one can do it for me. I must decide I want to get well.

What the actual what?!

This hit me hard and unexpected. What about Dave being the only lifeline I have? What about me working myself sick while they play? What about the loving support I need?

I was angry. When Dave told me, I stormed out of our apartment and briskly walked into the hospital, demanding to see Dr. Chang. She agreed to see me for 10 minutes, and I was left with a few lines to contemplate when I returned to the apartment:

"A drowning person often drowns the person who tries

to rescue them. You are going to get better. Dave and Sean need to be fine too."

As our vacation to Langkawi approaches, I know Dr. Chang is right. I see it, but I hate it. My irrational mind tries to rebel, but I hold onto her words and promise myself to do better.

Chapter 12
LANGKAWI

Monday, October 31 – Saturday, November 5, 2005
Langkawi, Malaysia

As promised, Dave takes us to another Malaysian paradise. We awake early on Monday morning and take a taxicab to the ferry station. A peaceful three-hour ferry ride later and we arrive at the party spot: Langkawi. Here, the beer is cheaper than the bottled water. So, it's Dave's idea of fun.

But what do I want?

I cannot wait to *sleep*. I'm not ready for anti-depressants, but I bring Dramamine and melatonin. These are evidently two drugs I do believe in. We plan some fun days of swimming, playing with Sean, eating, and foot massages.

We take a funicular to the top of a huge mountain and look out west over the Andaman Sea. While we are riding in the gondola, Dave takes one of the ugliest photos he's ever taken of me. But there I was in all my glory, pajama top over shorts, getting out into the warmth and sunshine.

Hey, I'm trying!

We race remote-controlled cars, fight off the monkeys and horned bills who invade our cottage, and we go for Russian food that gives me a reason to eat. Beef stroganoff, yum! Finally, we find the spot that becomes our regular pub, and we return several times. It's a tiny reggae bar along a dirt path that plays 70s American music and serves nachos.

We go hiking, play American football, and construct an obstacle course for our remote-control cars in our hotel room.

I lie around on the porch after we've run the monkeys off again. They're very adept at stealing sugar from the mini bar whenever a window is open. I pick up a newspaper left by the cleaners. The headline reads, 'Young women sold in China make their way to Thailand.' I read the article and ask God, "If I ever stop being crazy, will you let me help young girls like this?"

I go to the beach to think and to get some sun. As I am walking back up the steep hill, I think, 'You know, I so hated going to a new school in the middle of the year. If I am only able to save Sean from one bad thing in this entire situation, I can at least ensure he doesn't have to do that?'

For nearly a week, I slept 10 hours a night, ate my fill, and finally spent some time with my family. I got real rest and the negative thoughts in my head went silent. It was my first extended glimpse of what my life in Malaysia could have been. It's amazing how quickly I've recovered after that one week of rest.

Monday, November 7, 2005

After our trip to Langkawi, I return to Nocura with a smile, a tan, and some added weight. Glimpses of the real me are actually peeking through! Why didn't I just take a leave of absence? I can do this!

Shut up! It's over. You've quit, and it was the right decision.

When I look back over the previous quarter's result, it is absolutely ridiculous that I thought about ending my life over this small failure. With all the problems, we still achieved approximately 93% of our sales goal. *Who would believe I was thinking of killing myself over an A-minus?*

Now, to be fair to myself, expectations at Nocura are not like they are in grade school. 93% is not an A-minus at Nocura—it's actually more like a D and is reported with black on presentation slides. 98% is a C (orange), 100% is a B (yellow), and 100+% is an A (green). God forbid you achieve 90%. I think that's an F. I am sure this is extremely motivating for macho people who always make their numbers. But then there are the rest of us.

My head clearer after time away, I finally realize that I did *not* imagine all these things going wrong at the same time. In my few months here, the Executive Team was put on notice to turn around the region, I've been at least 10 staff short my entire tenure, and we had our quota doubled in my second week because the Small Business team joined us. Then there was the added India quota, and finally, Luke's departure after unheeded warnings and Juliana's instructions for me not to learn Luke's job. To top it off, I wasn't trained, there was no time to ask questions, and, as a Director, I had fewer chances at camaraderie.

Angry now, I summon up the courage to tell my folks back home that I'm quitting. I am now strong enough to face the shame and embarrassment. And even though I see a glimpse of what a little rest could have done to change things, it's too late for that. It's done.

-----Original Message-----
From: Janna Donovan
To: John; Jim
Subject: RE: HOWDY

John, Jim, thank you for writing me, calling me. Sorry to hear about your changing job situation. I know it is tough. I hope you'll find something even better.
I have thought of you and your families so much over the last few months. I've tried to think what you would do in my situation. You've been very strong and I, like you, assumed there was nothing that could get me down.
I just got so stressed and so tired and I couldn't think. Lots of things happened at Nocura to add to the problems... So after 3 months, I wasn't delivering, I let my boss know that I wasn't ramping up fast enough and asked for a leave of absence to get some rest and get my brain back in working order. Staff leaving and hiring freezes and the pace of the business convinced me I really could not take a leave, so I kept going, but I just kept getting more and more tired. So, mid-October I resigned, I just couldn't keep going.
I guess I feel a little justified. I finally got a week off with rest (everyone was off on holiday last week) and found my brain was coming back, I was able to think and take care of myself. If I'd taken that leave, it might have been different.
I have to be done with any looking back or self-pity. That is what is dragging me down. You know how it is.
Now I have to work until November 30 so here I go, back to the salt

mines. I can't let the last 3 weeks of work take me back down that road again either.

We haven't decided when we're coming home. Might be best for Sean to stay in school for a whole year. Will you please advise me whether Mom's condition means I should come home right away? Dave is going to talk to Darrel, but she's been trying not to worry or burden me, so want to get the right information.

I will write this all to Dad in a letter. I'm copying Jim so I can tell you both at the same time.

Thank you for your love and concern, we will rebuild and we will be home, please take care of yourselves and your families...

Janna

My brothers write back and tell me to come home immediately. God love them. They are doing what they have always done—defending me from anyone who dares try to hurt me. It is excellent to have two strong, dominant male brothers like this. It's probably why I was so attracted to Dave.

But they're not too attracted to Dave right now. They think he's keeping me in Malaysia against my will. Jim and John blame Dave. Dave blames Nocura. Other people in my family blame Malaysia and Malaysians. They don't know how loving and kind and generous the people in this beautiful country are. Malaysians are certainly not the reason I can't say no to a job I hate.

I am trying to figure out how I got myself into this situation without blaming everything and everyone. I am trying to accept my part. I am trying to not repeat the same mistakes, such as leaping before I look. I am trying to not move Sean just because things didn't work out, like my parents did every few years during my childhood. I've got the savings to just stay put. Why shouldn't I?

Tuesday, November 8, 2005

On the surface, my colleagues and team members at Nocura look very similar to me and one another. Most went to college. Most trained for their specific job. Most have families. Most people know how to act at work, and how to put up a façade.

A work façade can be a good thing, because it keeps others from knowing what we are hiding: Distrust. Envy. Shame. Guilt.

It's okay for me to hide how much I distrust some people and envy others. I don't want them to see that I feel shame and guilt. They don't know that I grew up with my share of chaos and that I blame some of this on alcohol, divorce, and dark secrets. That's none of their business.

Until now the chaos made me edgier, more aware and able to stand up to leaders who made decisions I disagreed with. I was resilient because of all I'd been through!

In some ways, I think I enjoyed fixing chaos at work because I was used to it. Work has always been a place where I've risen. It's helped me compensate for some of the immovable disappointments that have bothered me in other areas of life. *But they do not need to know all of that.*

It's the second week of November, and Adelyn Wei, a new employee, has finally arrived from Kuala Lumpur. She is to replace Luke and Richard—positions that have remained vacant for some time.

Juliana is here all week to help Adelyn, who is in charge of coordinating advertising. I set up a management system that works for the new team responsibilities. Business-speak abounds. I have always hated business jargon and I am surprised (dismayed) at how much I have grown to use it. I hate it with a passion.

The team is, I think, secretly shocked and angry that I've hired someone who is not from Penang for the high-profile position. It puts her at such a disadvantage, but I put on a brave face to support her. My departure is coming, and I must give her the best start I can, especially considering the circumstances.

Adelyn is a beauty with a strong resume and great presence. I like her instantly. I take her for lunch whenever I can, and she meets up with another friend from KL who already works at Nocura. She speaks to her family nightly and makes plans to return each weekend to see her husband. He stayed in KL to manage his family's law practice.

However, hiring Adelyn is the thing for which I feel the most guilt. In my heart, I know she is not an absolute fit for the job, but she is intelligent and switched on, and she was the most willing and confident candidate I could find. I try to recreate her resume and interview in my mind, searching for clues that tell me she will survive the difficult demands of this place when I am gone.

Then a harrowing thought dawns on me. 'Is that what they did to me?'

Wednesday, November 9, 2005

I stand in the shower at 5:30am and let the water pour over me as I try to gather up courage. It's still dark, but I am used to getting ready this early. I tell God, "Okay, I will trust you and I will trust Dave. I'll stay here as long as you want. I'm scared, but I will stay."

But it's only been three days back from Langkawi, and I can no longer sleep again. Although I won't take antidepressants, I want someone, anyone, to do something about my inability to sleep. Tara has already said sleep deprivation can make people suicidal, even homicidal. Maybe a little sleep would make the dark thoughts go away.

So, I write Dr. Chang again to ask her for help, trying to sound less suicidal than I am.

-----Original Message-----
From: Janna Donovan
To: Dr. Chang
CC: David Donovan
Subject: Advice on sleep
Hello again,
I understand you've spoken with David and want to thank you for your help.
I am back to a cycle of not being able to sleep. But I feel pretty "normal/positive" when I go to bed, no terrible thoughts, same during the day. Is there any sleep aid that I can take that's ok given my recurring depression?
Janna

She suggests I speak with the psychiatrist. But I trust her more. She's the one who has cared for me.

Tuesday, November 15, 2005

Another week goes by, mostly sleepless. As I look ahead to November 30th, my greatest fear is finally being home with Dave and Sean and "not being there."

I can't bear the thought of just sitting there staring into space as I've done so often with Sean on the weekends. This fear, and the knowledge that anti-depressants take two weeks to show any effect, motivate me to schedule with the psychiatrist.

If my last few weeks with Nocura are marked by side effects and headaches and fuzzy thinking, so be it. It can't get any worse. I may regret this forever if I get "addicted," but I have to do it. I have to be there for my son, so I schedule an appointment.

At the psychiatrist's office, I admit that I have flushed the anti-anxiety medication down the toilet, so he prescribes more that I have to take along with my new batch of anti-depressants. The dosage is very low, and I secretly plan to take half of what he's prescribed. He suggests I stay off the web logs and other websites that tell me all the dangers and side effects. He says I must enter this time of healing with a positive attitude. I have to listen to physicians and take what others say with a grain of salt. But trust has never been easy for me.

I write to Angelica, a Christian friend who's had difficulties in the past. She offers the only encouragement that a depressed person can really accept. It helps because she's a person who has been down and come through it.

-----Original Message-----
From: Angelica
To: Janna Donovan
Subject: RE: A big ol' secret...ssshhhhh!

As for your taking meds, I totally understand how you feel and promise to keep that secret until you reveal it to others on your own. When I was at a very bad point in my depression, my then-husband took me to a doctor at Methodist.

I felt like he was dropping me off there with the doctor and saying "can you fix this mess?" It was very de-humanizing. When I sat down with a doctor and my husband and I candidly discussed my feelings and my thoughts of suicide, the doctor accordingly prescribed medication for me.

That moment was excruciatingly painful; I cried and cried from then all the way home. It was like my biggest fear (that I was crazy) had been confirmed. I felt a lot of shame and fear and trepidation. Depression captures your mind and not only holds it hostage by negative thoughts, but it prevents hope from forming.

When I was very depressed another time, a friend shared a verse with me that gave me a whole new perspective on depression.
Here's the verse:

John 10:10 "The thief comes only to steal and kill and destroy; I have come that they may have life, and have it to the full."

In this verse, it refers to the devil as "the thief" who is stealing your joy by telling you lies in your mind (you know, those repetitive dark thoughts you think when you are depressed). And when you believe them, instead of God's truth, the devil steals your joy, kills your hope and tries to destroy your life. I think of what you told us many times: God is Truth. Seek His Truth. WORD!

I hope that gives you some comfort. I do know what you are going through right now. And all those hands that are reaching out to help...don't worry about which one to take or how hard it is to reach up and grasp one...just let them reach out to you, to pat your head, rub your back, or give you a hug. Just be still and allow Christ to administer HIS MEDICINE which is LOVE through the body of Christ...your friends, who love you!

Otherwise, your "keep going forward" plan is a good one. Just take each day as it comes, take your meds (it will help your thought process to get back on track) and know that I am praying for you for VICTORY over this!

Angelica

I wait until no one is around and go to the kitchen to cut the pills into quarters. I hide the anti-depressants from everyone, skulking around like a drug addict, but I take them. What a silly girl I am.

I invite Adelyn over for homemade pizza. She says her uncle is coming to Penang this weekend. She admits that the new job and everyone's expectations make her feel stupid. I tell her not to ever think that. She says, for the first time in eight years, she's having migraines again.

Oh God, what have I done to her?

Chapter 13
'TIL THE BITTER END

Wednesday, November 16th, 2005 - Penang, Malaysia

The new advertising agency prepares to take over the Marketing System. The Marketing System is prepared quarterly to plan how advertising dollars will be spent to deliver every call needed to meet the sales plan. A "man on the ground" from the agency will provide the detailed planning we will need to complete it.

I stay up late at night and I'm awake at 5:30am to work on this one last project with the agency. Dave is appalled.

The last time I meet with Mark Denning and all the other VPs who recruited me is during a divisional presentation. To this point in my career, I had never felt like the outcast that no one wants to be around. I'd always worked for and with the top, no matter if it was an established company or a startup. Now I am the pariah of the group, people ignore me, and even talk over me. So, I keep my head down and my mouth shut. When I do answer one question, I sound so quiet that I wish I hadn't said anything at all.

Afterward, I attend the mandatory "Manage to New Heights" Nocura training program provided to motivate managers and help with career planning. For the first time in over a month, I cry. I really was proud to work for this company. I had high hopes and dreams of making an impact as a leader for decades.

A reorganization is rumored and vaguely announced, but the details have not been outlined to all the staff. One person who is leaving is Haruto. He is being sent to the UK six months before his tour in Malaysia is supposed to end.

Haruto has given so much to the South Asia region and the individuals on his team, through his positive outlook and his unwillingness to quit in the face of negative news. So, in my opinion, that is going to be a huge loss to Nocura South Asia.

Haruto is given a very short amount of time to move to his new position. He is asked to report for work the following Monday in the UK. Before he leaves that day, he comes by my desk and points at a photo of me with my stepsister, Nina.

"Be that person again, Janna," he says. "Swear to me you'll leave this building and not stop looking until you find the light in your eyes again. Don't stop until you are your strong old self again."

The moment he leaves my desk, the email icon pops into the corner of my screen. Fear grips me as I see the subject line and the name of the sender. It is from my son's principal.

-----Original Message-----
From: Daniel Worth
To: Janna Donovan
Subject: Sean

Dear Mr & Mrs Donovan,
Just a brief note to give you words of encouragement.
I had Sean in my office this week to show me his maths work (a graph) on country of origin – he was clearly delighted to be here for praise.
In our weekly subject updates, I also noticed the swimming teacher recording how 'great' Sean had been this week.
We appreciate your ongoing support and are pleased with the progress we are seeing in Sean.
Hope you have a nice weekend
kind regards, daniel

We are at the bottom, and Daniel, our boy's principal, helps carry our precious Sean when we can't.

What gift can I possibly give this man who loves my son so much that he goes the distance with him? How can I possibly convey what his work means to me? If I were rich, he and his wife and children would never want for another thing in life. He has our undying loyalty. Got to find some way to let him know.

My family has been pleading with me to immediately return home to the US. I want to, but I find things to dread about both staying and leaving.

-----Original Message-----
From: Janna Donovan
To: Mom
Subject: RE: TGIF
Hi, MOM! I'm doing well. Have continued to exercise and take it VERY light at work so I can stay up. I'm eating more and look a lot better!!!!!!!!!!!!!!!!

What are you doing up so late/early? Your week sounds great, wish I was there to enjoy it with you. How are you feeling?

I've put the heavy thinking and decision-making on hold for right now. Just need to get through these next few weeks at work. Wish I hadn't told them I continue working till Nov 30. Oh well. Please continue to re-iterate to Jim and John how much I appreciate them and their love. Only the next month will tell if staying here and resting is better for me than moving home right away. I'm as anxious to find out as you. Regular appts with dr. will start next week.

Got lots of emails from friends in Houston giving me support and love. Lay-offs going on there in US so they were not surprised at my news, just supportive.

Need to write Dad or call him. Birthday parties and fall festivals planned this weekend. Fun and sunshine.

We can talk on Skype Sat morning 8 for me/ Fri 6 for you if you can?

I love you very much,

Janna

One of the worst fallouts from the six months of chaos is the level of anger, conflict, and pain in our relationship with our seven-year-old son. My inability to control myself means I don't have the confidence to discipline him. It seems like Dave is so focused on keeping me upright that he feels like giving up whenever Sean is out of control.

-----Original Message-----
From: David Donovan
To: Janna Donovan
Subject: just so you know

that sean hates me too. other than the fact he is sitting in his room looking for all intents like the character from 'the exorcist' let me tell you about picking him up from school today.

I went to get him about 3:00. this is the time we have come to a truce on. last week when i arrived at school to get him at 3:00 - i think on tuesday - he lambasted me publicly for making him sit by himself and wait "so long" for me. the very next day I arrived at 3:00 and he was angry because I came so early. I frequently sit patiently and let him play for 30 min to an hr before we come home.

So today i arrive at 3:00. I ask if he is ready to go, he pleasantly begs me to stay longer...i ask how long, 30 mins. I come back in 30 mins, half scared that his friends will have left and he'll be angry that he's had to sit around and wait on me. When I return at 3:30 I bring cookies from gurney plaza for him and his friends, he thanks me. Then I ask that we leave because I have frozen food in my pack that needs to get home, he throws a fit for the first 10 mins of the walk. I ask why he treats me this way when i gave him 30 more mins with his friends and then brought him cookies. i told him this sends me the wrong message, that being nice to him gets me treated badly.

Then later i go downstairs to drive the remote control truck. he wants to go too. i have a turn for about 30 secs. he wants a turn. after a few minutes I suggest we turn around so that we can drive back before the car runs out of juice. he says no (can't stop the fun), i ask for a turn, no, please may i have a turn, no, when can i have a turn, ignore, so i head to the elevator, he follows now, because the car is out of juice. We come upstairs, i download a pc game for him. he wants to play yu-gi-yo. i ask for the rule book. he gets a fake one. i ask for the real one. he says this is the real one, with increasing intensity he repeats and assures me this is the real one, i ask for the other, he escalates, he starts screaming, his face deep red because i will not accept the truth about the yugio rules. he's been in his room now for this entire email, maybe 10 mins and keeps coming and asking to come out.

i know this isn't positive energy for you, but know that you are not alone. you and i are in this boat together with sean, and we'll row until we reach shore. other parents and their children have been in this boat before us, we're not special in that way. i love you. see you soon.

-----Original Message-----
From: Janna Donovan
To: David Donovan
Subject: RE: just so you know
I am so sorry Dave. I wish I knew what the answer is. I don't know what to do to teach him to love.
I thought it was to continue with what my parents taught me "The world doesn't revolve around you, think of someone else once in a while."
What can I do but discipline him when he hurts you? I just feel like you get it in stereo when I'm having black sock days.
It's like dealing with a 3-yr old in a 7-yr old body.
Janna

-----Original Message-----
From: David Donovan
To: Janna Donovan
Subject: RE: just so you know
no, no, no. you're misunderstanding. this is not to "fix" him. this is to tell you that this is how it is. the answer is not to "fix" him, but to

continue to spend time with him and love him. we teach him every day. you don't need to discipline him for me. you need to love him for you. and what's a black sock day? and i resent the remark that dealing with me is like dealing with a 3 year old in a 7 yr old body.
DaveD

Why can't I see this the way Dave does?

> Tuesday, November 22, 2005

My final day at Nocura is drawing closer. It is only eight days away, *but I still can't tell anyone that I am leaving.* I hate it. I'd like to say goodbye. I've made relationships here, and I care about these people.

On top of this, I receive some shockingly harsh news from the service Nocura uses for visas. They tell me that, on my last day, my work visa will be stripped from me. My passport will be amended to reflect the immediate expiration, and I will need to leave the country.

I immediately email Dave in a confused panic. My heart is racing. Do I have to leave the country without anything I own but the clothes on my back?

So, I ask Dave to fly us out of here.

-----Original Message-----
From: Janna Donovan
To: David Donovan
Subject: FW: Cancellation of Visa
Importance: High
Dave, can you find a cheap airfare anywhere outside Malaysia for 3 tix by next Tues?

You might say I'm caught by surprise. I guess we can buy advance US tix that are changeable.
Janna

This is a purely poetic end to a Big. Fat. Nightmare. We've essentially been told to pack up and get the heck out of Dodge. No longer with Nocura? Well then, you're no longer welcome. It makes my stomach churn and burn with nervous rage.

We are asked for air tickets to confirm we are leaving, but after some research, we ask if the tickets can be for a bus to Singapore or Thailand instead. We find out that the buses travel in style, and we can make a visa run and be back in time for Sean to attend Sports Day on Thursday.

"Bus tickets? Oh…sure, bus tickets are fine," comes back the answer from Immigration.

The service had six weeks to let me know this info. I guess they had to freak me out one last time!

Chapter 14
DIGNITY, IN AN EXIT INTERVIEW?

Friday, November 25, 2005 - Penang, Malaysia

Arjun, the senior HR person who conducted my first interviews and my original site visit, is present at the end. He conducts an exit interview with me.

    I go into it not wanting to burn any bridges, but I also want to stand up for myself—a difficult balance to achieve. Arjun asks how the process could have worked better to ensure that I was a good fit for the job. I advise him against recruiting from other divisions of Nocura when recruiting from abroad. I say that the transition might have been easier if I already had a set of facts and experience to lean on. Then, he asks me what I truly thought went wrong. I give him three main takeaways:
1) Too low headcount
2) Too much change to manage with a skeleton crew
3) If I'd taken a medical leave of absence, it may all have turned out differently

He leans over the desk and asks for candid feedback on my direct manager. I am taken aback by his question. I tell him I don't have anything negative to say about Juliana. She has been a good manager and has been a caring leader throughout this entire situation. I'd told him previously how upset I was that she forbid me to learn Luke's job, but because I knew there was so much for a director to deal with in any company, I wasn't going to drop her in the grease because of that decision. Especially in an official record.

Then he asks the final question. He wants to know if it's possible that I oversold myself during the interview process.

I straighten my back, look him straight in the eye and reply, "Yes, Arjun. I put my best foot forward. But everything I listed about my previous experience was true. We all knew it was going to be a stretch for me. In every challenge previously, I always swam out of the deep end. I thought I would do that here."

Arjun tells me there is some feeling among the hiring managers that maybe I had too much winning in the past, that I haven't lost many battles during my career and I found it difficult to deal with here. 'Fair enough,' I think. Interesting concept.

I say to myself, 'So I should have failed more often in the past so I could be less bothered by it now?' I am not thinking in a sarcastic tone. I am actually contemplating the weight of that statement and trying to learn from it.

I know I shouldn't, but I feel impaled after the exit interview. I guess I expected him to collect my badge and my laptop and silently walk me out. I am caught off guard when he wants to talk for almost an hour. He explains that hiring and placing higher executives is a very expensive process. So, it is imperative that they find out all they can when things don't go right. I feel judged and scolded and whipped.

Dave emails and asks me if I can be laid off instead. He thinks it might help with paying the claw back or applying for some sort of severance package.

-----Original Message-----
From: Janna Donovan
To: David Donovan
Subject: RE: What about being laid off
I just asked Arjun and he said he wouldn't hold out any hopes for that. That it would typically indicate poor performance and make it much less likely that I'd ever be rehired (As if I'd be rehired now). He will get back to me.
Janna

-----Original Message-----
From: David Donovan
To: Janna Donovan
Subject: RE: What about being laid off
And is ever being rehired even a vague concern?

-----Original Message-----
From: Janna Donovan
To: David Donovan
Subject: RE: What about being laid off
Not really. But Wong Li just came by and said if I'm staying here, come see him if I want a job. weird.
Janna

-----Original Message-----
From: David Donovan
To: Janna Donovan
Subject: RE: What about being laid off
do what you gotta do.
Dave

Am I still holding onto a shred of self-respect? Do I need Nocura to help me with that? No, if and *when* I regain my confidence, I don't think it will happen in the corporate world.

Still, I'm bothered. Dave's "Do what you gotta do" comment seems flippant and petty. I'm the breadwinner in this family, and I have been for 8 years. I always think about how employable and promotable I am, and I'm still thinking about it during this completely screwed up time. As the coach said in the movie *Bull Durham:* "We're dealin' with some s*&% here!" I'm the one who's had to be the adult, while Dave's been walking in the sunshine and trying all the local food!

I also want to scream at how leaders pulled back support from my team and criticized them. We understand that our sales totals are small compared to the other countries, but I have left it all on the field, literally, and I can't play the game anymore.

It's like no one realizes this!

I'm reminded that I and my division achieved at 93% of our goal since I arrived, and I was ready to kill myself over it. Talk about a lapse in reality!

Wednesday, November 30, 2005

The big day has finally come—the one I've been waiting for. Quitting Day.

I do a little work, clear out emails and say goodbye to people. I want to go to lunch with everyone, but instead I must go to the Immigration Office to have my passport amended.

The man who does these things for Nocura employees brusquely asks me for our three passports. He says he doesn't need me but guesses I can come along if I want. We drive through winding streets of Penang to the office. I tell him, "I know I have to leave the country immediately," and he snorts a big laugh.

We walk into the Immigration Office, and he points at the chairs furthest from the clerk window and says, "Wait there."

As I sit, waiting for my passport, I think back to the cold New Mexico spring, that day in the snow when my mom told me a call was waiting. It seems like each interview, each party, and every goodbye was a waste. It took me ten months to get this job, and I've only kept it for five. Another brand-new experience and a very embarrassing fact.

He talks to the woman behind the counter in Bahasa, smiling and joking. A few minutes later, he comes back with a form for me to complete and *voila!* We do not have to leave the country until December 30th. School will be on break, and we'll be a little less overloaded with tension and fear.

I thank him profusely. I really needed that gesture on a day like today.

Chapter 15
IT'S FINALLY OVER: NOW WHAT?

Thursday, December 1 - December 6, 2005
Penang, Malaysia.

It's officially December, and for the first time in years, I don't have a job. I weigh 112 pounds, up from 103, have weird zits and a permanent crease in the skin between my eyes from scowling.

Whatever.

Unshowered and with no makeup, I decide to go with Dave to drop Sean off at school. I want to see what it's like. It goes against my Texas upbringing to go out without primping, but go I do!

Good thing, because it is Uplands Sports Day, which is a huge day for all the Primary classes. Parents come to see their children compete, the music plays, and the children win ribbons when they place in each event.

Sean steps up to the line for the softball throw, and the coach is 20 feet in front of him. As Sean sends the ball sailing into the air, the coach's head lifts toward the sky, and he watches the ball arc straight over his head and land 20 feet behind him. Sean runs out to mark his spot and holds the flag high in both hands for a picture-perfect moment. The shocked looks on the other children's faces makes Dave and me laugh excitedly.

Despite my anxiety, I begin to learn how to get around Penang. Before, I had Rafeeq take me wherever I wanted to go. I thought that being driven around would relieve or prevent stress, but I soon learn that's not the case at all!

I get in our little kookaburra with the steering wheel on the right side and find my way to the grocery store and back to the Immigration office by myself. As I do this, I gain a little clarity and independence—two things I've been sorely missing for months. Maybe I should have started driving sooner? Oy vey.

A few days later, on a Saturday, I get 8 to 9 hours of straight, uninterrupted sleep—something else I haven't done in months. When I wake, I don't pray to God for the desire to go on with life. I don't even yearn to stay in bed. I get up, and everything feels so...*normal.*

I love Dave and Sean. I get to watch Sean at Tae Kwon Do at his school, and Dave and I have a moment to just sit down and talk for the first time in a long time. We run into Sylvia, Sean's teacher, and she has the sweetest things to say about our son, his energy, and his love for learning.

On Sunday, fully rested, I watch TV and plan Sean's birthday party. I feel hope today, and I have created a healing schedule that I intend to put into daily practice: exercise, shower, Skype, buy food at the open-air market, clean house, and pray/meditate. I'm motivated now, but will I really feel like doing it when the time comes?

I read about Social Anxiety Disorder and the success stories of those who have overcome it. I visualize myself being okay and able to function without paranoia. Will the anti-depressants help with that?

Monday comes and I alternate between lying in bed and walking everywhere in Penang. "You have to get some sunshine on your skin. You have to get some light exercise to wake up your body. These will help with your depression," says Dave, trying to help me overcome my resistance. We walk to the grocery store, the bank, several shopping malls, and, of course, every day we go to Sean's school, a historic building on Kelawei Road. There, I sit on the dark, heavy, pew-like benches near the open-air badminton court, reading a Stasi Eldridge book while the kids chase one another around or play an upright piano.

So, as far as I can think, this is my plan for healing right now (I make a lot of plans):

- Walk
- Sunshine and warmth to thaw me out
- Read books from authentic authors who've been where I am
- Force myself to eat

All the walking and the less than robust appetite results in the loss of a few pounds. A week into being unemployed, I weigh 110 pounds. Not thin by some people's standards, but that is stick thin for me. I can still pull my pants on without unbuttoning them.

While I'm mostly enjoying myself, sometimes my skin crawls with negative thoughts.

Depression should be called something else. It feels like you have a combination of PMS, flu, and jetlag at the same time, all the while you're lying with your braces stuck in a green shag carpet that smells like a fraternity house party. Sometimes I can ignore it, but when I get up and move around, it's like walking around in quicksand.

What do I do? I want to go home, but I keep thinking about my biggest fear around this solution. I won't be able to stand the 30-hour flight without having a panic attack.

Even though I hate them, I think the anti-anxiety drugs could help. But what about when I get off the plane? My family and Tara wouldn't even recognize me, and there would be this cloud of anger around Dave. My family is furious because they think he won't let me come home, regardless of how much I explain that Dave is fighting for his sanity and Sean's stability. They are mad that I am the breadwinner. They are mad that I have fallen into the dark well of depression, partly because of overwork and exhaustion, and they're mad that Dave's unemployed.

It's such a double standard! If Dave were a woman and I were a man, would the wife be blamed for the husband's work burnout?

Tara is more reasonable, but she also wants to protect me. She reminds me of the day that Dave said, "If you want to have a child, one of us has to get a job." Is it a crime that Dave wanted to be home with Sean? Why won't anyone understand?

And then there's my dad. My dad is a boot wearing cowboy from Texas. He is the genuine article, even has a horse and carriage business in Galveston. Partly because he does not do email or Skype, I have not spoken to or exchanged correspondence with my father for six months. It's the longest stretch in my life, and it makes me very sad.

I write my dad a letter letting him know that I plan to call him on Christmas Day to celebrate a little. I warn him to keep the call celebratory, and to not complain about Dave and his lack of a job. I tell him that if he asks me to leave Dave and come back to the US with Sean, I will hang up. I tell him that Dave is the only father Sean is ever going to have and we are going to stick together, no matter what.

I go to see my counselor regularly, trying to unravel the mystery around my depression and anxiety. I know it is a fabric that I began weaving way before last July. It goes back a lot farther than that. I hit the roll bar of a dune buggy with my forehead when I was 14 years old. Could that have added to it? Was I six when the thing happened that I never talk about? My memory is fuzzy. Someone touched me in a way I did not understand.

No! Not going to blame it on childhood stuff. It's about being addicted to succeed at a job I hate.

So, how am I really? Well, according to Dr. Chang, this is how it looks:

- Depression is mild to moderate (oh, wow, if this is moderate, what must the real thing feel like?)
- My occupational standing is that I have taken a positive step toward self-preservation by quitting
- Socially: I am not isolating myself, which is a great sign
- I am functioning as the mother of my family
- I am forcing myself to eat (always wished for this problem, but now that it's here, it's weird and scary)
- Mentally, my concentration is still shot

I get invitations to go out with new friends, but I don't know who to trust with my secrets. Now that I'm more available, Dave and I argue over how to raise Sean. I can't believe I'm considering staying here with only Dave's input. But could I truly connect with my family members back in the US and trust their advice?

The whole time I've been in Malaysia, they have worried and talked amongst themselves about my big life decisions. Even before traveling overseas, I felt defensive when they criticized me, but I did take their advice—sometimes without proper reflection. Now I see how my inability to say 'no' and stand up for myself was and *is* dangerous to my health. Don't they see I have no boundaries and I get taken advantage of?

I go see Renee. She's an American woman in my building who has experienced the pain of transition and gone a lot further down the dark hole than I have. Renee has also recovered, and I want to learn from her.

She gives me simple advice:

Experience touch as much as possible. Find what your triggers are and avoid them. Get hobbies. Don't fight the meds. Visualize them working. Visualize getting better. Hugs for Sean, hugs for Dave. Take advantage of the next six months! Get a routine. Same thing at the same time each day.

But I find it hard to take her advice. I reason that being disconnected from reality seems like the meds talking, not me. I decide on my own to slowly taper off the anti-anxiety drug. I just take smaller doses each week, contrary to the original prescription. Still, I stay on the anti-depressants.

Sundays are hard. I go to the Penang International Church near our high-rise. The service leaves me longing to be as strong in my faith as I used to be (or remember myself being!). Other Christians seem so energetic, full of happiness, and functional. I don't know how to engage with them. I don't even think I'd want to be around me right now!

"God, help me be happy for others. Happy that they're not going through this weirdness," I pray. I write in my small pink journal:

"I actually feel as if I was singing to You today, God, for the first time in a long time. The message was full of hope and humanness and second chances after awful things.

Then, I have a social anxiety attack right there in church and want to leave. What are they thinking? What are they saying? What do I look like to them? Why do I worry so much about what others think of me?

God, I miss you. Please help it to be You I want and not just Your forgiveness. I want the peace, the love, and the joyfulness I used to have.

But why is it God's problem to fix? Didn't I paint myself into this corner? Almost all I do is tinged with guilt. 'Should have, should have not,' greets most decisions. I must think about the poor and be compassionate to others because we have so much."

How do I stop making this everyone else's problem? I want to be babysat and held and massaged, but this is not me! How do I walk my way out, ignore my feelings, distrust all my emotions? How do I exercise with no calories in my body? I am seriously afraid I'll be hospitalized if I continue to go deeper into depression.

I just keep repeating, "God is the Sovereign King, and He loves me," as a way to push away my despair. However, because church turns out to be one of my biggest triggers to fear and sadness, Dave and Mom ask if it wouldn't be better to take a break from going.

How am I supposed to feel the touch of God if I cannot even go to church and worship? But it's true...when I do, I feel like damaged goods and hate myself a little more. It's painful. It's possible I'm trying to find a formula, a spiritual explanation, for a physical problem. This makes me even sadder.

Then, just like that, as if nothing is wrong, I get up, put on some different clothes and some makeup (always a Texas girl's best defense), and I go to out to dinner with Dave, Sean, and our friends. I feel light and alive, but I know it's a temporary reprieve from what's to come.

The next day, I visit Dr. Chang again. I tell her about the suicidal thoughts. She asks why I have not attempted it, and I say "Sean and my mom. I could not do that to them." She asks me to carry photos of them in my wallet and look at them whenever I think of hurting myself. She calls the continuous loop of negative tapes in my head depressive rumination. I need to observe the thoughts in a non-judgmental way and accept them.

See, I thought ignoring them would help me cope. Acceptance is another thing altogether.

Then she asks, "What have you been doing with your days?"

I say, "I mostly stay in my room and read books and articles on how to recover from depression."

She laughs, which I do love about her, and then says, "You have only been off work for six days and you are busy at it, trying to get better?"

She says, "Stop trying so hard. Don't focus on the disease or fight it. Accept that you have it. Stop thinking, 'When will I get better?'" But I am impatient and a little mad that I'm not going to change overnight.

What can I say? I am ruled by my expectations, which can be very unrealistic and unfair. My perfectionism and my expectations of myself persist. GET OVER IT. IGNORE IT. Engage with Sean. Snap out of it and stop struggling with the additional pressure to get well faster.

To my mind, not fighting it is the scariest thing she could have advised. If I accept depression, won't it wrap its tentacles around me and never let go?

Wednesday, Dec 7, 2005

I take my journal of daily details with me to visit my psychiatrist.

It seems the medications are just decreasing my appetite further. I can't think of anything I really want to eat, yet I have to exercise to increase my levels of serotonin. Most people have enough serotonin to naturally maintain a positive or neutral outlook on life. Why not me? I'm stuck in a loop, impatient for a solution.

It's a week after leaving Nocura, and our landlord requests a meeting to understand our plans. She needs to know if she should begin the process of renting out our place.

Even though we have signed a two-year contract, she is willing to let us out of the contract after Dave explains our situation. She is caring and understanding and comes to our house for lunch.

That morning, just as she is arriving, Dave reminds me of

the warmth and the sun and the rest we'll both have. And just like that we make the decision to stay in Penang for another six months. It is great fun to tell her and to have a final decision made. Dave and I hope this will help me turn the corner.

Why did I think it was going to be so hard?

Because I make everything way harder than it has to be.

How do I feel? I ask myself this a lot, patting around on myself mentally, as if looking for broken bones or bullet holes. I can fight off the thought demons and lies and move about. But I cannot cry. These thoughts churn through my mind constantly:

'How am I going to get better?'

'When am I going to get better?'

'What are my rights?'

'What did I do wrong?'

'What did *they* do wrong?'

Actually, I can't care about that right now. I am sick to death of words. I can't read or watch a movie because every thought, concept, song, lyric, or line act as a trigger for dark and negative thoughts. Even an uplifting movie like *Sea Biscuit!*

Get positive! Get grateful!

I don't want any more words. My brain is on strike. I need to take in the world differently, by the conduit of experience.

My perfectionism has been blown away. But I will not allow myself to say that any good came from this experience. Others may state it as a healing kind of thought. But it is a grotesque one to me at this stage. It would mean that I am okay with this nightmare. I put my entire family through this, without anyone else pushing me. From the first interview to the last day, I made this happen and everyone else had to suffer along with me as I failed, time and time again.

"Please God," I say to myself. "Please don't make any good thing come from this. I can't bear the thought."

Saturday, December 10, 2005

I have one of the worst nights since this entire thing began. I was up at 1:00am after taking the meds at 9:30pm. I am restless and anxious in bed. I have negative thoughts and memories. I suddenly have more energy, but that energy translates to anger and disappointment. I am mad and I point all the anger inwards. The thought of hurting myself floats into my brain again.

I am much better when daylight comes. The thoughts of 'I'm not going to make it' seem to dissipate with daylight. I force myself to get up and eat a bigger breakfast than usual.

To my surprise, Saturday is a white sock day. I help Sean with a big school project on Africa. It takes all day and I love how much I let him do the poster, crooked title and all. He keeps pasting cut-out magazine photos of cows and lions. When he doesn't want to continue, we make cookies. *Together.*

I talk to my mom. It's very upbeat and I avoid triggers. I walk for 40 minutes and play football with Sean in the park near Midlands.

I decide to go to my old General Manager's Christmas party, very afraid of my motives and unsure what a Nocura party will trigger. Despite my anxiety and worry, I dress up in a short black cocktail dress, laugh, and have loads of fun. After it's all over, I feel ready to stop managing my depression like an addict, thinking of it constantly, picking at the scab like I know I shouldn't. I need distractions, don't I?

I hope distractions will make the triggers diminish.

Sunday, December 11, 2005

Breakfast and church, no panic attack. Have I been putting my faith in my faith, instead of putting it in God?

Got to keep going. Who cares if I'm just going through the motions? Would God have me not go through them at all? Would He have me not take Sean to church? I can't let the fact that I've messed things up so badly stand in the way of giving Sean a spiritual, moral base—a relationship with Jesus.

I am getting more and more upset when Dave, after he's had a lot to drink, brusquely disciplines Sean. What can I do? I have to object; I must do something. I have to make it a peaceful house again…now! I thought I was taking care of myself and my family when I decided to stay in Penang for six months.

Then I remind myself that if we'd gone back right now, we'd be disoriented with no house, no car, a new school and new teacher for Sean, and no anchor.

I'm not sure what to do for fun or which friend to ask out. Every expat we know is traveling home for the holidays. I ask Bianca, a friend from Chicago, out for sushi. I'm very excited to be going to lunch during the day, like someone playing hooky from a job. I'm anxious I'll be triggered, but it turns out to be fun.

I tell myself what they tell the strongmen of American football as they push against one another on every play: "Just keep chopping your feet." This reminds me to just keep trying things. Taking small actions have been my only periods of relief. Of course, that's interrupted by moments of hiding in my bathroom and lying down on the hard floor.

I have trouble listening to others and their concerns without it weighing me down. Except for Sean. I can listen to him all day long. That's as it should be.

Sunday evening, Dave and I fight vehemently over something stupid. I write to Dave after the fight. I tell him this is the mixed message I hear:

"I am not feminine enough to please you. My body is not the right shape or size. I am too castrating for you. I don't give you enough sex. You don't give compliments, romance, flowers, or any other tender messages, so I don't expect them. Foreplay is 'You want to fool around?' Sex is out of duty because that's the only duty you expect.

"You want me to be more of a woman, but how can I do that when I'm being a man? I'm a ball-buster, but I need to keep making my 100K salary if one of us is going to work. You genuinely think I make it all about me, in life, in our reality. But you spend all day living on your own schedule, feeding your inquisitive mind, critical of others who take chances you wouldn't take.

"I'm supposed to change, but you are allowed to say, 'This is just the way I am.' This arrangement is comfortable for you until you want a voluptuous, sexy wife."

I hand Dave what I've written. He shouts back, "All this is only true in your head! I have always, *always* been attracted to you, always wanted you, except maybe when you got too skinny! I wasn't trying to tell you how much money to make.

I just wanted you to get paid what you are worth…for the risk you were taking! We are best friends, always will be, but I am not going to sit around making my life miserable just because you are miserable."

Argument over. I withdraw without much of a comeback. I look out the window at the sea and remember Dave's demeanor when we first met. He had a confidence that I wanted. He rolled with my ups and downs, but he wasn't the type to let someone boss him around either. His refusal to go along with everyone else seemed to say, "Like me or don't. It's all good."

After some time passes, I laugh and think, 'Pretty clever of him to sneak in that backhanded compliment about me being skinny. My man knows how to make it right with his wife!'

I am just so tired of being angry at myself. I'm ready to take a break from despair.

Chapter 16
WILL AND DESIRE TO CHANGE

Thursday, December 15, 2005 - Penang, Malaysia.

It's a glorious day in Penang. The sun is out, the breeze is coming off the ocean. Dave and I walk around Georgetown, the city center of Penang Island. We gawk at the facades of the white-washed colonial buildings and enjoy the noise, bright colors, and busyness. My head is clear, and I have energy. I am happy.

When we return home, it turns into a difficult afternoon. I start to feel lonely and sick and wonder if I should just give up. God, it feels so alone to go through this without a girlfriend to hold your head in her lap. I just want someone to ask me over to her house.

Then, as if I've received a gift from the heavens, Renee, the American friend who gave me advice about surviving depression, invites me to her huge, beautiful apartment.

I think, 'This is it! A girlfriend who understands!'

When I arrive and we get through with small talk, she leaves the room and returns with a small gift. She says, "I made these Christmas candles for my friends, and I'd like to give you one too."

Oh God, plunge the knife in my gut and twist it.

What I heard: She has friends. But I am a charity case.

People do not realize how raw your heart is when you're depressed. I take the big, luscious candle, choke back the tears, and leave. Luckily, I am alone in the elevator because my mouth gapes open. I feel like saying, "Keep the candle. It's not the candle I want, Renee. I want you to call me your friend and invite me over or out, and not be ashamed to be seen with me." I know I'm a mess, but I've done this for so many people in the past. Can't it be my turn? When do I get to be the mercy date?

I still don't want to eat anything. I think, 'Don't antidepressants increase your appetite?' I have always enjoyed eating. As a chubby kid, sugar cookies and Kool-Aid were my favorite part of Vacation Bible School. I remember it like it was yesterday! In Malaysia, I have found some things that are high in calories that I love— mainly mango lassies and Tandoori chicken. When I can't think of what to eat, I add Ensure to a big glass of milk. Sexy!

Saturday, December 17, 2005

I excitedly prepare for Sean's 8th Birthday Bash. A surge of happy energy rushes over me, and I feel as if none of the past six months has happened. I hang balloons everywhere, put up a Happy Birthday sign and put out fun plates for the table. I then pick up five boys at early release because it is the last day of the school term. We go back to the high-rise and eat hotdogs—chicken ones for Sean's Muslim friends—as well as their favorite crisps.

I'm having as good a time as I can remember since arriving in Penang. The boys are fun, polite, and easy to entertain. I feel myself bursting into laughter as we host some fun games like smash-someone-else's-balloon, pass the parcel, and freeze-statue (must freeze when music stops. Last one moving is out!). Sean is the only one who takes things a bit too far. They LOVE the prizes: squishy balls with lights inside that blink, pull-back racecars, and other stuff I succinctly label as "happy crap."

Dave takes them all down to the pool where they play two hours of dodge ball. Sean once again takes things a bit too far and is sent upstairs for ten minutes. Then everyone races back upstairs for remote control cars and a huge order of Domino's pizza.

We give Sean *The Game of LIFE*. It is his favorite of all the presents. Big smile!

The boys get ready for bed as we drag out a queen-sized mattress for them to sleep on in the living room. Three bodies line up sideways on the bed and the others sleep on the couches. I read Dr. Seuss to them, and then *The Night Before Christmas*. It is amazing to read it to children who've never heard the poem. They love it, and they all brush their teeth and go to bed giggling.

It's a rocking good party, and I go to bed happy, calm, motivated, and clear. I get a great night's sleep, with no twitching, no heart palpitations, no night sweats. Sheer heaven.

I wake up, and decide I need a routine of things I can do.

Maybe I can volunteer at school, or volunteer somewhere else?

Sunday, December 18, 2005

I'm afraid to go to church, but I go anyway. I want to be forgiven for overreacting to stress, giving in to fear, and telling God that things should go according to *my* plan.

After the service, I tell Craig that I don't feel close to my son. As a stern father might, he says, "Well, that's the way it is. The only thing you can do is start tomorrow to change that." It feels harsh at the time, but by the time I get back to our house I realize it's a very effective slap in the face.

Ready to listen, I ask Sean if he wants to stay or go back to the US. He says he doesn't know what he wants. I ask him what his feelings were when he first arrived in Penang. He says, "Nervous. Things were broken up. I thought we were in a bad life." I ask if he feels that way now. He says, "No." My guilt won't allow me to believe him. In my confusion I think he is still mad at us for bringing him here.

Sean continues to test many boundaries with Dave and me. He says he will do things that are gross or dangerous to scare me. I go on the internet to read about 8-year-old behavior and find that it's not as outlandish as I am catastrophizing it to be.

This is the situation in which we find ourselves: foreign country, disagreement over how to discipline a challenging child, my mind/emotions coming back but not all there, not much structure/no real job. We have six months to decide what to do next. Do we stay, go home, or go elsewhere?

Everyone is asking me where I want to live and what I

want for the future. I want to tell them that, three weeks ago, I could not even decide what I wanted to eat let alone plan out my family's future.

Truth is, I'm not sure I would trust what I want, even if I had a clue what that was. What are my desires? What do I want for myself in terms of personal growth?

After some thinking, I decide I want a life evident of love, connection, balance, boundaries, artistic expression, and a place for myself (a home). This is a formula for thriving anywhere. But can a will and desire to change coexist with full acceptance of myself as I currently am? Not sure. At this point, I'm tired of the mental gymnastics.

All I do know is that we are going home in the summer regardless of whether we decide to return to Malaysia or stay in the US for good. I don't want to return to Malaysia, but I am afraid to push my opinion, because Dave is the one who'll need to be employed in the US. I just *can't* right now. Moreover, I don't want to stomp my foot and say, "Let's go home!" I'm worried I'll have a difficult time transitioning back. Besides, I think I've done enough foot stomping for now.

At this moment, I need to focus on getting better. I schedule many fun things in Penang for Christmas and the entire month of January: parties, joining, connecting, and helping out at some local charities.

Sunday, December 25, 2005

We have Christmas Day planned at Jodi and Craig's.

Christmas is a wonderful day, even though there's not much under our three-foot tall tree decorated with slightly tacky, dime store decorations. That's all I could find!

We open presents and Sean gets the *Narnia* Gameboy game and some money from my mom. Dave's Mom, Babcie (Polish for Grandma), sent clothes and a cool game. We give Sean *Pictionary* and some clothes and books.

We prepare to go to the party at Craig and Jodi's apartment. Dave covers a big, beautiful ham with fresh crushed ginger, pineapple, and brown sugar. Then, he scores it in a crisscross pattern with the boning knife and places a clove in each of the corners. He cooks it very slowly and the smell spreads throughout our floor.

I make appetizers and a pie with frozen Haagen-Dazs ice cream without thinking we need to transport it on an 80-degree Fahrenheit afternoon. Oh well! No time to change my plans now.

We carry this all to the 15th floor of Craig and Jodi's high-rise building, overlooking a lush pool and the tropical sea. As we enter, we are welcomed by the lavish Christmas décor, twinkling lights, and holiday music. It is entirely fitting for Jodi, who is an artist accustomed to hosting Christmas in the tropics. Guests from almost every continent are there, all very interesting people. We are all dressed as if it's the summer because, well, it is.

Sean has fun playing with the other kids while we help set up and cook. Craig samples the ham and I feel like we are finally home. We sit down to a long, inviting table, and after a wonderful prayer from Craig, we dig in.

I inwardly shake my head. I almost said no to this party because they had invited several postcard-perfect families. I thought comparisons and triggers would abound. What a waste of mental energy!

After the meal, Jodi and I walk back to the kitchen to

retrieve the pie but talk too long. The pie mostly melts. Dave is disappointed in such a lapse but forgives us. 'Tis the season to celebrate Grace and our Savior's birth after all.

When we get home, I call my dad at our predetermined time on his Christmas Day—10:00pm for me, 10:00am for him. I'm a little on guard, ready to be defensive or hang up. But he amazes me by saying, "I liked what you had to say about Dave, that he's the only father Sean is ever going to have. I support you." Then he asks, "So how did you let yourself get to the point of a nervous breakdown?"

What's the deal with my family and the phrase "NERVOUS BREAKDOWN?"

Wow. It sounds so pathetic and weak. *Ouch.* I laugh out loud and say, "Well, it wasn't exactly a nervous breakdown…"

Yes, it was. I laugh again.

Then he says, "Whoever was your boss and did that to you at Nocura better not let me catch them in a dark alley. I have a bull whip and I will use it on him some day. These big corporations think they can just use people up and spit 'em out when they're not of use any longer."

My mom and Dave echo my dad's sentiments. They want revenge and they want to sue. But who do we sue? It's hard for me to find an individual person to blame at Nocura. My colleagues and my bosses both in the US and Malaysia are all good, hard-working people. I heard horror stories about slave-driving, angry bosses in high-tech manufacturing, but I never encountered them in my time at Nocura. We did what was needed for our team to succeed. We put in the hours required. As they say in *Master and Commander,* one of my many favorite movies, we did it "subject to the requirements of the Service."

No, I wasn't going to sue. I let myself get to this point. I always erred on the side of saying yes. It was me who was slightly neurotic and OCD, and that, combined with overworking and too much worrying, meant that I was burned out before I ever set foot in Malaysia. I was the one who decided to take a job for which I had little preparation. Naïve and full of juice, that's me!

Everyone has limitations. Being honest about them was not a strong suit for me. But facing them is a must if I'm going to survive this and find another way to succeed. I've got to learn to play within myself.

Chapter 17
THE BOY'S GOT NO FEAR

Friday, December 30, 2005 - Koh Lipe, Thailand

For New Year's, we go to a remote island called Koh Lipe on the western side of Thailand in the Andaman Sea.

Hat Yai is the border town we enter as we leave Malaysia. Walking down the street, I look up and there is a Nocura Printer sign. Dave's old T-shirts and a cool camera bag are all reminders. I can't get away from the word, the brand, the name. I tell Dave, "It's like dating someone famous. After the breakup, you see their face everywhere." He laughs and says, "You couldn't make it work. He just wasn't your type."

We travel by bus to Pak Bara, the port where we will catch a boat to Koh Lipe. While we wait for our boat, we have breakfast in this tiny open-air restaurant. We drink strong coffee, eat a huge fry breakfast with eggs and sausages, and I think, 'Thank you, Brits! For travelling everywhere and making this dish so popular in tourist resorts!' We are so happy at that moment we proudly take our photo with the cook and server like they are family. We are in love with everyone. It's like being drunk, but without the alcohol.

Sean, now eight years old, asks Dave to get him a drink. Dave smiles and says, "Why don't you get one yourself?" Backpack slung over his shoulder, Sean wanders off to talk to the guys who work on the boats. Then, despite not speaking Thai, he walks into the store and buys himself a drink. When he returns, Dave dubs our strong, fearless son "The Intrepid One." He has no fear.

The boat ride to Koh Lipe is loud and smelly, but it's a clear contrast to what we encounter when we arrive to the island paradise. Emerald water, white sand, stucco cottages, and thatched huts. Lush trees and their large green leaves hug all the paths, some with creamy white or orange flowers. We clean our room of sand and ants, then strike out on a hike.

Within two or three minutes, it feels as if we are the only three people on the island. We arrive to a deserted beach, its white sand shore leading softly toward the water. Across the strait, there is a larger untouched island rising majestically out of the ocean. Sean and I walk toward the water while Dave takes photos. I lie down at the water's edge, lean back, and slide my feet into the sand. I close my eyes and let it all out.

I'm safe. I'm warm. I'm with the ones I love.

Tuesday, January 3, 2006

We arrive back home in Penang and watch Dave's alma mater, the Texas Longhorns, beat the USC Trojans to win the National Championship in College Football.

We are shocked to find out that we can watch the College Football Championship game live here in Malaysia. Best. Game. Ever! So many spine-tingling moments. Especially the defense's fourth down stand to give the ball back to Texas with 2:09 left to play. Vince takes it in on a fourth and five, as Blalock blocks for him. A two-point conversion and USC runs out of time. Texas Longhorns win!

We jump and scream and seriously consider running out into the streets.

No one can truly understand what this means to us. It's not that they don't care. It's not that they don't go crazy for sports—many Malaysians go crazy for World Cup Soccer and the Europeans love tennis and hockey. It's that they've never heard of Vince Young or what it means to gain 467 yards. They don't know what a Longhorn is. They can't begin to know what it's like to win this way in the Rose Bowl and put this grudge match to bed.

Yes. Yes! A win and we get to watch it live from 15,000 miles away!!!

But my elation is quickly deflated by an email. It makes me close my eyes with guilt and hang my head.

Adelyn's uncle came from KL to see what it would take to help her return. He wants to rescue her from the nightmares and migraines she's been having.

-----Original Message-----
From: Adelyn
To: Janna Donovan
Subject: Hi Janna
Hi Janna,
How have you been?
I've left a message on your machine wishing you and your family happy holidays. I don't know if you've already gone back to the U.S. Btw, there was a friend of yours who wanted to get in touch with

you, and I gave her your mobile number as well as this email. Sorry, I forgot her name. Hope she was able to get in touch with you.

Janna, I just want you to know that I have already given in my resignation to take effect end or beginning of February. I had to learn Luke's job and stay there every night until 11pm for about 3 months until it was more under control with the Ad agency (they want me to extend but I can't).

Thank you for being a friend here in Nocura. You can always get in touch with me at my personal email address if you want to.

Best Regards,
Adelyn

I write back and apologize, asking if there's anything I can do. I am sad, but I am resolved. I cannot let this take me down into despair and self-loathing. Self-pity is not going to get Adelyn's old job back. I must get better, so I never put anyone through this again. In Alcoholics Anonymous I believe they call it "having a selfish program." This flight is still experiencing turbulence—I have to keep my oxygen mask on.

Wednesday, January 4, 2006

It's the last time I will see Dr. Tan, my psychiatrist and prescriber of meds. He leaves me with two requests:

1. Continue to see Dr. Chang, my counselor and psychologist.
2. Contact him immediately if I encounter more than three of the items on the depression list of symptoms for 14 days in a row.

Later that same day, I go see Dr. Chang. My notes are

really a jumbled mess:

"I am lovable. What happens if I'm not lovable?"
"Being ultra-responsible leads me to care for others. Is that a bad thing?"
"Self-esteem is not the same as confidence or always doing what is right. Self-esteem is knowing one's limitations." Not sure about this one.

I still haven't completed the "These are the memories I want" assignment Dr. Chang provided me, so she asks me again: "What are the specific memories, events, and feelings that you want to look back on when you are 90 years old?"

Hmmm...Sean's graduation, his wedding, his children. Going to the beach with Dave for our 50th Wedding Anniversary. Coming back strong from this embarrassing time.

I tell her that it is taking two of us right now to raise one kid. "Each of us is like half a person!" I complain through gritted teeth.

She says, "So what?"

This is my favorite phrase she has taught me, and she says it a lot. If it takes two of us, that's how many it takes. So what? *It takes what it takes.* I hold on to this during my times of self-doubt. I need this phrase to swing the pendulum of my thoughts away from my persistent *there's only one right way to do things.*

To my surprise, we talk about not meeting quite as often going forward, and I wonder what that means for me. Does she think I'm doing better?

She also pulls out "The List" and asks me to see her

immediately if I encounter signs of depression. Dr. Tan and Dr. Chang have coordinated their delivery of my care very well. I feel loved and cared for by both of them.

Thursday, January 5, 2006

The most unlikely thing I've done during this time? Cook. I'd never learned to be a true cook because I was always trying to stay slim. Anorexic habits and cooking don't mix was my reasoning. Why think *more* about food, right?

Plus, Dave took over cooking from Day One of our marriage. I baked, especially during the holidays, but getting home at 6:00pm on a weekday and then beginning to cook dinner? Seriously, shoot me in the eye. My motto was, "If it takes me longer to cook it than to eat it, that's a waste of time." I'm embarrassed to say what I ate as a result of this logic.

After Dave and I were married a short while, I called my mom and said, "You'll never guess what Dave has done! He's made me feel like less of a woman by taking over the kitchen! He insists on cooking all the meals!"

My mom replied, jokingly, "Call me back when you have something real to complain about!"

So, 18 years after abdicating the role of cook, I'm interested again, and I email some old friends about it. It sounds cliché, but it is helping me to connect to the nurturing energy found in my mom, aunts, friends, and friends of friends. Unlike at other moments of my life, nurturing encouragement is what I want to overdose on right now. Plus, well...*food!* I take it all in. I slow down and enjoy the sensations. I put aside the desire to rush, get agitated, or fret

about the outcome when delving into a new recipe.
It takes what it takes!

Tuesday, January 10, 2006

We're in the costume business now. It is Book Week at school and there is a parade followed by a party. Sean is asked to come as a favorite book character, so he chooses Peter from the *Chronicles of Narnia*. We put together a costume, not really getting the point that it's *Sean's* creativity they are looking for.

We plunge forward, have a seamstress make body "chain mail" by using silver silk and black tulle as the mesh layer over it. We find sheet aluminum at the hardware store for the armor and shield! We make reticulating armor for the arms.

It looks amazingly close to the real thing. It is way over the top in a ridiculous laughable way, but it is fun. I vow to let him do it himself next time.

Before we go on another of many school breaks, we receive good progress reports for Sean. They describe Sean just as I've known him: highly intelligent, curious, and great at concentrating when the subject interests him. He is outgoing and learning to coordinate with others.

I smile a big smile of hope and calm and love. That boy is so unique.

Wednesday, January 11, 2006

I'm feeling the forward progress, and it's as startling as it is amazing.

I've begun my Bill of Rights for different areas of my life.

It feels ridiculous to think that other people hold and practice these "rights" with no problem. They don't have to scribble reminders on sticky notes and paste them on their fridge.

But, hey, that's why I'm in counseling... to learn, right? This one is about work.

Work Bill of Rights and Responsibilities

I have a right to take care of myself physically and mentally.
I have a right to rest.
I have a right to make mistakes.
I have a right to desire things.
I have a right to ask for help.
I have a right to ask questions.
I have a right to take time.
I have a right to training.
I have a right to transition time.
I have a right to say, "I don't know."
I have a right to have an opinion.
I have a right to disagree.
I have a right to change my mind.
I have a right to ask "why?"
I have a right to enjoy the things I work for.

My leaders tried to convince me of some of these rights. I just could not hear them.

Dr. Chang wants me to create more Bills of Rights with my mother, Dave, and other family members in the US. However, I am not good at failing other people or telling them no, but I have to. Dave and several other family members don't seem to realize that they want me to set boundaries with other people, but not with them. *But I have to.* Always seeking acceptance from others has proven costly, even before coming to Malaysia.

Finding self-acceptance *seems* like an antidote. So, let's see if I can do it.

Tuesday, January 17, 2006

I attend the first International Women's Association (IWA) meeting of the calendar year in Tanjung Bungah. I look forward to making all kinds of new friends. It's a dream come true. I joined a similar organization in Tokyo 13 years prior, and since arriving in Penang, it's been something that I've wanted to do but couldn't find the time. So, here I am.

We meet in the hotel ballroom, surrounded by fragrant tropical flowers and ornate furniture. Women in suits and dresses stand in groups throughout the room. Five or six of us stand together and talk casually about how we got to Penang. I explain how I am ready to have some fun.

When I tell them I quit my job because I wasn't happy and became a ghost of myself, they say, "Didn't you know it was going to be like that?" I shrug my shoulders, put up both hands, and make a "What can I say?" gesture.

Another woman asks, "Can job stress really change your appearance that much?" Several of us in the group turn to her, and in unison say, "Yes!"

Our tables are set with china and heavy tablecloths. We listen to the speaker and eat the ladies-who-lunch meal which is yummy. It's a mixture of Malay, Indian, and European favorites.

It feels great to talk about my troubles in the past tense. It is easier to admit them. I am struck with an unmistakable feeling:

I'm moving on.

Thursday, January 19, 2006

I make a very showy dessert for dinner at Liz's. It is still odd to socialize with a person who's high-ranking at Nocura, but hey—I'm evidently getting over myself. I want this dessert to be good *and* beautiful because she has been nothing but good and beautiful to me.

I use a recipe I wrote down when I was 17. I was with my Gran, dreaming of owning a restaurant. It is an Italian custard dessert, Zabaglione, served in tall crystal flutes. Ours are glass—good enough.

I mess it up, but I take it in stride. I find out it's surprisingly fun to just keep breaking eggs, trying it again, and getting it wrong. In the end, I make something amazing.

It dawns on me that this is not like me. I usually feel so rushed and have to get it right the first time. The old me would have given up if it didn't go well the first time. Sound familiar? Bye-bye perfectionism. No more ruining my life!

23 years after writing down the recipe, I finally eat it for the first time. It's weird and wonderful. "Try, try again" has never been my style, but look what I accomplished! It's the small things that bring me so much joy.

It takes what it takes.

Monday, January 23, 2006

I go see Dr. Chang. No need to weigh in this time. Four weeks of parties has fattened me up just fine. I ask her how I can help Sean be kind, to perceive himself as kind and good, and to not sell himself short.

She says, "Anything you can learn you can unlearn." He will learn in specific circumstances to accept himself. He will learn that he doesn't have to be perfect.

I must allow him to fall and pick himself up. Only then will he know that it's okay to fall.

Dave has a blog with a whole group of followers from all over the world. There is a serious change of tone in his entries over the last few weeks. They show just how much fun we've been having. It's as if we are healing five months of heartache with five weeks of fun.

Seriously, my head is spinning. We were made for this.

Tuesday, January 24, 2006

It's Chinese New Year, so I make carrot cakes with cream cheese frosting and give them to our landlord and next-door neighbors. I also make one for Janet, Liz's executive admin at Nocura, who's become a very good friend of mine. The cake's rich texture, sweet and salty frosting, Asian spices, and walnuts are very popular with everyone who tastes it. They look a little shocked, to be honest.

Naturally, Dave loves the Chinese New Year fireworks, and writes about them in his blog.

CNY – Dave Donovan
Submitted by admin on Mon, 2006-01-31 8:55.
Wow, what a week. Chinese New Year (CNY) is like nothing I've ever seen. You cannot imagine the vast quantities of

fireworks that were detonated here in Penang. It boggles the mind to consider what it must be like in Singapore, Bangkok and beyond comprehension what must happen in China or Taiwan.

Monday, February 6, 2006

We go to a remote island with no cell service, no roads, no cars. Don't get me singing the theme song from *Gilligan's Island*. It couldn't do justice to this place. Yes, the rats frightened me at first, but the games, laughter, and open-air, bar at the center of the island make it all worth it.

Thailand is our new happy place. After we get back, Dave can't stop raving about it on his website.

Paradise Found – Dave Donovan
Submitted by admin on Mon, 2006-02-06 20:55.
A few thoughts about our week. We spent most of the holiday in Thailand on a wonderful and beautiful island called Koh Kradan. We shared our journey with Sean's friend Joshua and his family. The eight of us rented a van and driver and left the driving to them. We stopped for Thai pineapples along the way and gorged ourselves for two days on some of the best pineapple I've had in years. On the island we joined three other families all with the common bond of having children in The International School of Penang (Uplands).
Returning home, we were caught in CNY traffic at the Thai-Malay border. Traffic was moving so slowly that we hopped out of the van and went shopping, bought dinner and some fruit, ran ahead to the duty free for some cheap liquor and got back into the van just as it was our turn to line up at immigration.
As we arrived in Penang, I was glad to see the electronic smart

highway sign showing no wait time on the Penang bridge (longest bridge in Asia, 3rd longest in the world). And it occurred to me that the smart highway signs here are better than the ones back in Texas. We're so third world in the US.

Caught the Superbowl this morning. Started at 7:00am. What a sloppy game. Penalties, fumbles, dropped passes, dumb mistakes…pretty much the same as every Superbowl that New England doesn't play in ("Belichick's still a god"). And if you're betting, my money's on Wales to win the Grand Slam in Rugby.

An email from Tara comes in while we are traveling. It is just the thing I want to see—light, bright and real.

-----Original Message-----
From: Tara
To: Janna
Subject: Get a coke
Do you want to go to Sonic with me a get a Coke and a jalapeño hamburger? We could roll our windows down and talk loud.
Miss you,
Tara

-----Original Message-----
From: Janna
To: Tara
Subject: RE: Get a coke
Man, that sounds good! Tater tots or onion rings? Can't decide.
Can't wait. Daydreaming the other day about living in/near Houston again because it would be easier to see you whenever you come to Tejas.
:o) Janna

Saturday, February 18, 2006

Zero anti-depressants today. But I will take one tomorrow. I've started to alternate the days. Feel ready to try life without them.

I'm planning to exercise six times this week. Tennis today, lunch soon after. My appetite is *way* up. Egg sandwiches, brownies, four slices of pizza and ice cream. It goes down great, but then I wake up at 3:00am with a stomachache and Dave fighting off mosquitos, so I go to the guest room.

Thankfully, I have no work in the morning. I sleep in late.

Writing now just to track that I'm not sure it was being OFF the anti-depressant that caused my sleeplessness. I think it was just that I ate too much, like a little kid at the state fair. Piggy pie!

Tuesday, February 21, 2006

The clouds are gradually going away. I feel like Robinson Crusoe when he discovered goats and grain on his island. I am a satisfied and full human. I'm whole again. I want to be aware and raw and ready to love. I don't want to go back to how oblivious I was before I felt all this pain. C.S. Lewis explains what I want to *avoid* in the 1940 book, *The Problem of Pain:*

"Everyone has experienced the effect of pity in making it easier for us to love the unlovely... The beneficence of fear most of us have learned during period[s] of 'crises'... My own experience is something like this. I am progressing along the path of life in my ordinary contentedly fallen and godless condition, absorbed in a merry meeting with my friends… or a bit of work … a holiday or a new book, when suddenly a… headline in the newspapers that threatens us all with destruction, sends this whole pack of cards tumbling down. At first, I am overwhelmed, and all my little happinesses look like broken toys. Then, slowly and reluctantly, bit by bit, I try to bring myself into the frame of mind that I should be in at all times. I remind myself that all these toys were never intended to possess my heart, that my true good is in another world and my only real treasure is Christ… by God's grace, I succeed, and for a day or two become a creature consciously dependent on God and drawing its strength from the right sources. But the moment the threat is withdrawn, my whole nature leaps back to the toys… God has had me for but forty-eight hours [but let] Him but sheathe that sword for a moment and I behave like a puppy when the hated bath is over—I shake myself as dry as I can and race off…"

I don't want the immense fun to diminish my awareness of how Jesus has seen me through all of the dark times. I don't want the healing to distract me from my ability to feel others' raw and very real pain—an ability intensified by this scary experience. And I don't want to forget that success and "being somebody" are great toys, but they don't compare with the experience of God being here with me, by my side, loving me. I also want to give Him *credit* for seeing me through all of the good times, having also made them a part of my life!

Wednesday, February 22, 2006

I meet with Dr. Chang. I weigh 127 pounds, but there's some muscle there! I've been lifting 50 pounds on different machines three times a week, then walking 23 flights afterward. I've tried to run them a few times, but it still might be a little out of my wheelhouse. That'll come!

The doctor and I go through a checklist of the relationships and other things in my life: Mom, Dave, rumors of Nocura job offers, sex, sleep habits, and eating habits.

I tell her a story that involves me driving our kookabura. Dr. Chang is shocked. "You drive in Penang!?"

"Yes, I've been driving since I quit Nocura. Dave and I figured it would be best to let the crazy one of us drive here."

No offense to Malaysians or Asians, but the traffic here is organized chaos just like I've heard Rome or Nairobi can be. I have just the right amount of guts and assertiveness to get where I need to go without making others slow down for me or get angry. So, I'm the one who drives.

Dr. Chang and I talk about my sinking spells, and she asks, "Janna, do you think you're hypoglycemic?"

"Oh yeah, I always have been," I reply. She says that experiencing "mini depressions" during the day is very common and that keeping my blood sugar regulated is a big priority if I want to remain positive and strong.

I tell her my Bill of Rights as it applies to my family.

Rights and Responsibilities with Family

I have a right to be different from you.
I have a right to disagree.
I have a right to live in a way you don't understand.
I have a right to live in a way you don't agree with.
I have a right to be happy in my life even when you are not always part of that happiness.

Reading them aloud is difficult. They took a lot of courage to write. But they are needed for me to accept myself and get better.

Thursday, February 23, 2006

It's so exciting to finally do things we've dreamed of doing.

We are hosting a Japanese high school student for a two-week homestay in March. We spend some time prepping the place for another person. It's still early, but Dave and I are thrilled with the opportunity to be of service to someone.

We also volunteer to put together a brochure for our international church. We want to help expats find a church in Penang full of people who understand what they're going through. We decide that we'll also help Craig and Jodi on some other things—about five hours a week each for Dave and me. They've been kind and generous to us, so it's very cool to be able to do something for them.

We've started playing tennis on Tuesdays and Fridays. It feels like a huge victory to go back to the site of my biggest panic attack and just have fun. The court is shaded until about 11:00am, so we definitely appreciate that! I'm having fun just enjoying myself, not trying to take a lesson or do it perfectly. It's such a fun sport to do with someone else. So is walking, which we do a lot, but it sounds more "athletic" to say you play tennis, right?

I make plans to read to kids at the School for the Blind and to voice record newspaper articles for the adults to listen to. I feel a connection to the school because it was opened by members of the Lions Club International service organization. My grandfather was a Lion back in Texas.

Sean is asked to try out for a team of athletes who will compete for his school in the FOBISSEA (Federation of British and International Schools of Southeast Asia) competition in Thailand this May. It feels like a big deal because he is one of only five boys from Year Three who is asked to try out. He is asked to compete in four areas: track, soccer, swimming, and tee-ball. Mostly we love it because he'll train after school with the coaches four times a week and then try out for the team after a lot of instruction and help. He already stays late at school each day for an hour or more with his friends, so it's really perfect.

The other four boys who've been asked to compete from Year Three are all in Sean's gang of five friends. We had most of them over for Sean's 8th birthday party. We really like their parents, which is a bonus because we'll travel to Thailand with them if Sean makes the team. TOO FUN!

I go to lunch with my friend from Denmark. Her name is Emma, and while she's a nurse back home, she is a stay-at-home mom in Penang. She's heard what I've been through, and she tells me about the rough time she had adjusting to Penang. It is very touching of her to open up to me about the sadness and exhaustion she felt as a travelling nurse.

I immediately decide that I want to get together with her every week. She is so open and *available* to me, and unlike most people here in Penang, she says yes when I ask to spend time with her. This is huge. It takes me back to a Friday night in high school when I was finally accepted by a gang of girls I thought were really cool.

Friday, February 24, 2006

I can't believe it.

Several colleagues from Nocura contact me about returning to work there. My former Sales General Manager and the Director of Procurement call to inquire. Even Haruto Ideka contacts me to talk about working for his UK team while based in Penang.

It's like a virus running through Nocura. The emails don't stop coming.

A former US boss, Michelle Gardener, also calls and asks if I'd like to be a US employee based in Penang. Michelle wants to talk at length and privately at our home when she visits us here in Malaysia. "I want to know what the hell happened that made one of my top performers leave the company completely," she says.

I smile. It is nice to have someone who remembers me back when I got stuff right.

I say, "They didn't twist my arm to come work here, Michelle. It was the other way around. I just didn't know how to care and not care at the same time."

My most recent boss from Nocura US emails to see if I'd like my old job in Houston. I seriously ask myself, "Should I go back to Nocura US to get back on the horse that bucked me off?"

To be honest, I'm a little surprised. They want me even though I'm a quitter?

That makes no sense. I'm confused. I think to myself, 'Maybe getting out of a dangerous situation is not the same as quitting after all.' *Hmph.*

Saturday, February 25, 2006

I go out for dim sum with five members who reported to me on my Nocura Malaysia team. When they call and ask, I immediately say 'yes!' even though I am somewhat afraid of what it will be like.

They are already there when I arrive. They are excited and surprised. So delightful, so full of joy. They look at me with such pride and pleasure, their heads cocked to one side. They say, "You look so good! You're...you're..."

I cut them off and say, "I know, I'm fat! And you love seeing me fat! Isn't it great?"

We laugh and I get to hear how everyone is. We linger longer than all the other lunch guests, unaware of the time because we are engrossed in inside jokes and loud laughter about the previous fall.

How am I laughing about it now?

Is this me figuring life out? Is this me growing up? Is this the restart of a life full of love, connection, balance, and a place to call home?

Yes. I am less wannabe, more somebody.

It is fantastic. They are fun. I am fun. The food is delicious. Who doesn't love dim sum?

Sunday, February 26, 2006

It seems my thriving social life is a little threatening to family who wants us to return to the US as soon as possible. Via Skype, Mom says, "You're going to meet so many great people you'll never want to come home."

I grin and say, "Everyone told me to go out and have fun."

She says, "I didn't know you were going to have *that* much fun!" We share a smile and a big laugh.

I've waited a long time to stop overworking and have fun. I want to stop putting off life so I can be who everyone else wants me to be.

No, I want to be who *I* want to be. But they might just be one in the same.

Still, despite all the good that's been happening around me, the inevitable has finally come. It's time for boundary-setting with Dave. I've come 15,000 miles around the globe and figured out my boundary situation with bosses and my family of origin. Now it's my turn with Dave.

Bill of Rights and Responsibilities with Dave

I have a right to ask that something be different. I don't have the right to demand it.
I have a right to feel what I feel. I will express it honestly without having to get mad first.
I have a right to make mistakes. I will talk about them without getting defensive.
I have a right to take time. This will help me be more decisive.
I have a right to transition time. I want to be game for every adventure. Gimme a minute!
I have a right to say, "I don't know."
I have a right to disagree. I want to grow up and have this be a non-issue.
I have a right to change my mind. Ditto previous one.
I have a right to light up an "Off Duty" sign above my head when I need rest.

Dave accepts these rights and admits where he has been forceful and domineering. He also reminds me that he's asked me to stop worrying about disagreeing with him and to ignore his opinions and picky rules when I need to.

Because Dave likes to call Sean the "Intrepid One," I look up the word in the dictionary. It's an adjective meaning fearless, adventurous. It derives from the Latin word *intrepidus*, formed by the combination of the prefix in- (meaning "not"), and -trepidus (meaning "alarmed").

I decide I'm moving closer to being intrepid—unafraid of being honest with the person closest to me.

Chapter 18
PARTY TIME!

Wednesday, March 1, 2006 - Penang, Malaysia.

Sean is such an interesting little man. He's raising money for Habitat for Humanity by baking a ton of my special recipe cookies and selling lemonade. He sells a lot of cookies to the older kids at school, carrying around a stash in a sturdy purple lock-top container.

He has let us know that when he grows up, he wants to be one or more of the following:
- FBI Agent
- Accountant
- Architect
- Chef
- Doctor
- Car Designer
- Dog Breeder

Monday, March 6, 2006

First full day *without* anti-depressants. Headache, PMS, dizzy.

No more fear of them. They have helped me get "out of the woods." And I'd take them if things get this bad again.

I notice Sean being left out in the school pickup line. Two of his best friends are leaving together for a sleepover, but there's no time to feel sorry for myself or Sean. When I get home, I ask neighbors Nicky and Oliver and their two kids to dinner. We sit down to a fine meat-laden meal. I laugh, others drink, and I love our new Australian friends.

Hanako, our foreign exchange student, is here from Japan and staying with us for two weeks! We're showing her a fun time while she improves her English. Her parents send the most beautiful gifts! We haven't taught her Texas words such as "fixin' to" or "ornery" yet, but it's on the to-do list.

We all go to Oscar Night at Sean's school, which is a debut for all the student films created at Uplands Penang International School. Years 6, 7, and 8 have a Movie-Making Club, all with their own films, and the crowd votes for winners. They ask all who attend to arrive Hollywood style. Dave and I dress in evening attire. I wear a long Dior knockoff and Dave puts on his favorite black Italian suit. The films are very good and inspire Sean and the rest of us!

Sunday, March 19, 2006

I feel terrific and strong. I am living a very good life in Penang. I'm calm and sane and clear. I'm amazed at my new freedom—a freedom that was always there but seemed impossibly out of reach. I especially like not explaining myself to others. Old habits die more easily than I was led to believe.

With time to breathe—and the clarity that brings me—I sincerely contemplate the unexpected job offers from

Nocura. But I decide I shouldn't go back. It's time I realize it's not for me.

Still, I find it ironic that I molded myself to the corporate world for 20 years, and then saved enough money to stay here and finally be myself.

Not much more time to ponder it; I'm late for art class. LOL! I'm a cliché and I don't care.

As I walk into art class, we are asked to explain the art we've produced from the week before. While waiting to talk about my sketches, out of the blue I think, 'How can a person be afraid of being big and strong? Why do we play small?'

I see this in my classmate, Alexis. In addition to being the best artist in our class, she is interesting and intelligent with an unassuming, natural way about her. But when she explains her work to the class, she is shy and deprecating. Eyes downcast, she tosses it off as rubbish. I think, 'God, do I do this? Am I afraid of the things that are incredible about me?' If I am, it's got to stop.

I'm part of a small group of women that get together every Wednesday. Most of them teach or coach at a local boarding school. We're talking about who God meant us to be.

I share more than the others. I get real quickly and I regret it. Then I think, 'Don't worry, they're younger than you, not yet loosened up by failure. They might not want to reveal their most vulnerable selves to the others, because they are co-workers.' As for me, I am used to talking to a therapist.

Besides, do I care what these women think of me? I am alive and well and getting the kinks out of my life. I am playing with house money, having gambled with my own sanity and lived to talk about it. I cannot, *will not*, go back to worrying about what people think. No more shame masquerading as humility. Today, serious conversations, connecting, and self-discovery are exciting to me. My intuition, insight, and compassion are back. I love it!

Jodi, our pastor's wife, has been a lifeline for me. She has led two different book studies of Eldridge books. Both are lessons I needed to learn and repeat, then learn and repeat. For one exercise, she asks us to ponder the question, "How do I reflect the glory of God?" I am supposed to write down all the things that make me who I am.

-----Original Message-----
From: Janna Donovan
To: Jodi & Craig
Subject: hi, Jodi, wanted to share thoughts
Here are some things I have thought about myself over the last 2 weeks as I discover how I reflect the glory of God.
I wanted to share them with you since I can't be with you on Wednesday.
Thank you so very much for helping me on this journey! See you Saturday. Let me know if you need me to bring something BIG.
Who I am:

- A Force to be Reckoned With
- Loyal, Initiating Friend
- Loud Laugher
- Bossy Show-off
- Party Planner Extraordinaire
- Cool Costume Creator
- Closet Tai-Tai Lady
- Fanatic Football Fan
- Post-Wannabe World Citizen
- Pleasing Wife
- Fun Mom
- Borderline Genius
- Tomboy Cowgirl
- Fearless Fighter
- Aggressive Athlete
- Delicious Dessert Chef
- Sincere Student
- Post-Perfectionist Realist

I don't hear the audible voice of God, but writing this list, I sense more how He loves people, how much He delights in them, and how much He loves and delights in me. I'm not sure I've ever stopped long enough to think or experience that. Rest is *so cool*. Ahhhhhhhhhhhhh.

Tuesday, March 28, 2006

Dave writes on our family blog about the fun we're having in Asia. His story in late March is the one that lets everyone back home know that we are staying in Penang for at least another year. *Yikes!* Repeat after me: "Stop feeling the need to explain yourself!"

Cambodia – Dave Donovan
Submitted by admin on Tue, 2006-03-28 12:43.
Every three months, we travel somewhere in Southeast Asia.
As most know, this past fall under mountains of stress and heaps of anguish JaDo axed the Nocura connection. After some soul searching and much financial consternation we decided to remain in Penang until June so that Sean could complete the school year. And then a funny thing happened on the way back home.
As JaDo made her way back from the dark side, the light of Penang began to shine brightly. The boy began to fit in, even excel in school and in sports. Me...well I've always had a thing for SEAsia and an insistence for spelling it this way. Somewhere along this journey the path became illuminated and we realized that our future would be tied to Penang and its International School for some time to come.
In order to follow this newly shone path we are negotiating for

new living digs, a semi-d (semi-detached, duplex to you) in Batu Ferringhi, the beach suburb on the north side of Pulau Pinang. We have committed to at least one more year here. We will again evaluate the options next spring and make the decision anew. The only scary part is this. We have two sets of friends who have told us that they too came here for a couple of years and decided to stay with the decision reevaluated each year. One couple has been here six years, the other fifteen.

This leads to the question, how does one live in Penang without employment? And the answer is I don't know. But we're about to find out. Does anyone know the rules for cashing out an IRA? But more likely is the strange but possibly true rumor that I will work for AMD, Intel, Dell, Motorola, Infineon or someone like that. We've also considered that there's no good tex-mex within 500 miles, so maybe there's a Taco Shack franchise in our future. But then again there's always that problem with cheese. Maybe we should move to the highlands and raise dairy cows. Any ideas? Your suggestions are both welcome and appreciated.

Saturday, April 8, 2006

I'm going for lunch with my old Nocura Malaysia team. Dave comes along this time! There are so many of us that we have to get two large round tables. Sixteen of us scoot in, eight at each table. The restaurant is small, cozy, and fancy. Red napkins in wine glasses, golden decorations. The dishes are truly delicious—especially the seafood.

It reminds me of the first dinner when Juliana welcomed me. Wow...full circle. I'm excited on the outside and dramatic and weepy on the inside. Is this really happening? Are we here, being included and welcomed by these friends?

No time to zone out! They're trying to talk Dave into ordering the sea cucumber because it will bring us such good fortune. Evidently, it is normally served at weddings for this very reason. I scrunch my nose and ask them if it's good. They say, "We don't know! We just order it for good luck. Hardly anyone ever eats it!"

I pass. Dave, of course, cuts off a big, globby bite and starts chewing, grinning from ear to ear. Everyone loves it and starts taking photos. I stand on a chair to take the entire group's photo. So much fun! So much joy.

Sunday, April 16, 2006 - Easter

At Easter service, Craig asks for people to come to the front of the room to share stories of when Jesus showed up when we needed Him most.

I go to the microphone and explain when Craig walked 40 minutes in the pouring rain to help me with my broken heart and confusion. I tell them, "I was making million-dollar mistakes and failing very publicly. Honestly, I don't know how famous people stand it!" They laugh. I thank Craig for showing up and teaching me how to lighten my emotional load. I tell him that, on that day, he was there for me and that is how Jesus showed up.

Just before I leave the microphone, I smile and say, "You know, I wish I'd failed sooner in my life and seen that it didn't kill me. I am going to survive!"

Saturday, April 22, 2006

Later that week, we travel to Siem Reap, Cambodia. There's

the three of us plus Liz and her son. Dave captures the trip, filling his blog with details of dusty roads, trendy spots, and a sad history. He is awed most by the grandeur and the gravitas of the impressive religious buildings.

I have less mature tastes. My highlights are visiting Templo Ta Prohm, also known as "The Jungle Temple" from Lara Croft and *Tomb Raider* fame. I also relish my time eating at the Mexican café called Viva. I take a photo of the quesadilla. It's so close to the real thing!

Houses of the Holy – Dave Donovan
Submitted by DaveD on Sat, 2006-04-22 12:28.

Flying from Penang to Siem Reap on AirAsia (unbelievably low fares) we spent our Spring Break in the Home of the Gods, Angkor Wat. Following the advice of our travel guide (lonely planet Cambodia) we sat in the front of the aircraft to help us speed thru immigration. Upon arrival in Siem Reap we drive from the airport to town, nothing but luxury hotels, many in various stages of development. This is a boomtown.
Old Market is hopping but the street's not paved. Trendy night clubs, exquisite restaurants, hard scrabble pubs, the old wet market (hence the name "old market"), dust and lots of it, mixed with the hawker stalls and street smells of Cambodia, all with the lingering quality of somehow having been French.
But one is never far from the tragedy of the Khmer Rouge and the civil war. One can dine in fine French restaurants for $10 per person including a good bottle of French wine but be no more than three steps from a landmine victim with no legs asking for a few pennies to help him get by. (The fact the US won't sign the land mine treaty is beyond barbarity.)

The party starts around 10 as the European and Americans spend their travel cash on $1 beers and $2 cocktails. The dancing goes non-stop and lasts until dawn, when people hop on board a tuk-tuk to travel to watch the sunrise from the back steps of Angkor Wat, the largest religious building in the world.

And from the hallowed wall of Angkor Wat to the impressive mountain temple of Prasat Preah Vihear across the valley to the carved riverbed of Kbal Spean to the jungle temple of Ta Prohm, the entire basin of the Tonle Sap is littered with hundreds of temples in various stages of disrepair. The scale is awe-inspiring, the workmanship is alien, the sense of timelessness incomprehensible.

If you ever have the chance, make the trip. It is truly a pilgrimage that is more than worth the time and effort. You don't get to see things like this but rarely in a lifetime. Personally it ranks with Iguaçu Falls, the Atacama Desert and floating in the barracuda vortex off Sipadan as the most spectacular places we've been.

As always, thanks for playing, DaveD

Chapter 19
BANGKOK THEN BACK TO THE BEGINNING

Wednesday, May 10, 2006 - Penang, Malaysia

We return from Easter Break ready for one more month of school. I'm happy to see how much my recovery plan has changed since it was just:

1. Stay alive
2. Don't freak out!

My list of things that will keep me on the sunny side of the street has begun to solidify. They are:

1. Maintain my relationship with God—Him the loving Father, me the beloved daughter
2. Protect my sleep
3. Exercise, even if it's a walk
4. Sunshine
5. (HALT) Don't let myself get Hungry…

6. ...Angry
7. ...Lonely
8. ...Tired
9. Very little to no alcohol
10. Forgive everybody for everything

Friday, May 12, 2006

The time has finally arrived for Sean and his friends to compete in the FOBISSEA competition in Thailand, and the entire trip is full of adrenaline, tears, fears, and screaming at tee-ball umpires.

At eight in the morning, on the day of their flight, we see off Sean and 30 of his teammates. They have cool shirts and yellow hats and 30 duffel bags with each of their names embroidered across them. As they pile in and the bus pulls away on Gurney Drive, Dave and I stand facing the ocean with tears in our eyes. Our son has worked long and hard to get to this point, and he is on his way to something big. Four days a week for three months he's stayed after school and practiced in the Penang heat. We hope he sees it was worth it no matter what happens.

There is no way we would miss seeing the competition. Later that day, we arrive at the airport for a one-hour flight with a 5:00pm departure time. Unfortunately, the plane is delayed, so we sit with friends as we consume wine purchased in the duty-free store. This turns into more wine as the delays keep popping up on the flight board. At 10:00pm, we roll down the runway and into the sky bound for Bangkok. Yawning, we land and arrive to our inviting hotel which is far from the venue. Dave always has to stay off the beaten path. Oy.

Saturday, May 13, 2006

We arrive a little late to the first morning's swimming competition because of the long car ride through Bangkok. Dave and I miss the opening ceremony but are ready poolside as the morning's swim competition begins. Our school's first competitor, a girl, steps onto the big box to start her race. I am breathless with the emotion that fills my throat as we parents cheer even harder for the children whose parents cannot be there. I think, 'Wow, if this is how I feel when it's someone else's child, how will I feel when Sean gets up there?'

Sean is switched at the last minute to swim in an event he doesn't often compete in. He climbs onto the box and looks out with such anticipation. 'He has never jumped off one of those boxes!' I think. But when the gun sounds, he runs into the water and I half laugh and half cry, seeing him giving it his all. Sean makes up four lengths but it's not enough to medal. I'm still so proud of him.

We survive, but the surges of adrenaline, the heat, and our late arrival the previous night have caught up with us. We invite one of the dads to slip away and enjoy some good food. He and Dave have a cold beer with lunch. What a couple of perfect moments we have with him, laughing and talking about international life, away from what's familiar.

We return to the field to watch our boys play tee-ball in a sped-up tournament. Dave and I are some of the only parents who know or care about the rules of tee-ball. I'm convinced this sport is only included because the Japanese and Taiwanese are an integral part of the FOBISSEA federation of schools. They want their children to prepare for baseball later in life.

We do not expect to win, but Dave and I are Americans to the end, questioning calls and asking why the runner did not tag up before going on to third. Daniel Worth, the headmaster and committed sports coach, hushes us with a smile and we walk away and try to let it go. It's just hard to watch the boys lose.

Sunday, May 14, 2006

The next day is much different. Dave and I walk part of the way and then catch moto-taxis to the Thai Army Stadium for the Track and Field events. I've been waiting a year to take a moto-taxi in Asia. We each have our own motorcycle driver, but my guy is the only one who knows where we are going. So, Dave's guy has to blaze through Bangkok traffic to keep up and make sure he doesn't lose us.

Traffic stopped? No problem—we squeeze between the sidewalk and a van. Then we scoot over to the center stripe and whiz between stopped cars and oncoming traffic moving at a pretty good pace. I instinctively squeeze my knees in so as not to bump cars on either side, even though I am already narrower than the bike's handlebars.

We notice that the drivers have helmets, but we have none. Oh well, you only live once. I might meet Jesus before this ride is over! Who needs to be on *The Amazing Race* with the life we are living?

During the track events, Uplands kids begin to win their races in the Bangkok heat. I get sick to my stomach thinking how discouraged Sean will be if he doesn't win. He's younger than all the others, and he's running against boys who are two years older after all! Then, as we watch our son fly down the 100 meters of track, Sean wins his first medal. Then he wins another two—one for running and one for throwing a softball.

The silver medal that brings a smile to everyone's face is won by our team of four "Mighty Mites." Three of the four boys on the 400-meter relay team, including Sean, are actually in Year 3, but they compete against Years 4 and 5 boys. As they climb onto the podium, each boy from our team is a full head shorter than the other boys. Sean wears all his medals around his neck, stacked and clanging when he walks. With hindsight twenty-twenty, other parents admonish me for worrying that Sean would come home empty-handed.

It's the definition of fun.

Dave and I try to enjoy watching as Sean finishes the football (soccer) day by only winning one game. They beat the only unbeaten team, which is glorious, but odd. Sean and his teammates go back to the Radisson to prepare for the Saturday night kids-only disco. Dave and I are free to get foot massages and visit an internet café to prepare for our next trip.

It will be even bigger and more emotional than the one we're on.

A trip home to the US.

Tuesday, May 23, 2006

There's no place like home. So much so that we plan to take Sean out of school early to embark on a 9-week visit.

However, we have been warned that going home to the

US can be a huge disappointment. Family may not be around, and friends may expect us to drive two hours to see them even though we've just endured 40 hours of air travel and layovers.

Saturday, May 27, 2006 - Saturday, July 29, 2006

Our experience is the complete opposite of that dire prediction. We are greeted with two family reunions in West Texas, just weeks apart, complete with a tennis tournament at one and water-skiing and lake camping at the other. Several weeks later, close friends throw a July Fourth Party in Houston and invite many of our friends. A day after that, my world is perfect with my friend Tara home on Texas soil. We enjoy a loud heart-to-heart talk at Good Eats.

Then we're on to spend time with Dave's brother and family, followed by my dad in Galveston. We have a daily diet of BBQ, Tex-Mex, and burgers, and I've got a serious wardrobe malfunction, but a very happy heart. The trip's best meal is the migas for breakfast at El Jardin in Galveston, Texas. I weep as I eat them. Not really, but they are delicious.

We round it out with a trip to Dave's parents' home in Louisville, Kentucky, and take in the horse races at Churchill Downs. The next day we complete honey-do's (kind chores or projects) for Dave's parents. Our perfect timing even allows us to see our busy nieces and nephews. Finally, we head back to Houston for more non-stop emotional highs, seeing people we have loved for 15 to 30 years. We make sure to slip in a regular queso intake at Pappasito's.

I make a trip west of San Antonio to meet Angelica at a local café in an old house. She's the one who helped me not feel so weird in the darkest days, because she had traveled before me on the crazy train of depression and lived to tell about it. She thinks I'm going further on to West Texas to see family. I love telling her, "No, you are the only reason I drove four hours into the middle of nowhere." Smile. Lavishing time on people is a great thing. I vow to do it more often.

One day, as I explain to friends the highlights of how I came to leave Nocura, the conversation I had dreaded finally happens. Sean speaks up for the first time about my leaving Nocura and says, "Mom, you were naughty. That's why you are not there anymore."

I am calm and I smile as I say, "Sean, I wasn't naughty. I told them that I didn't want to work there anymore because I was spending so much time away from you and Daddy. I didn't know how to do my job. I did it to protect myself. That's not naughty." He seems satisfied with the answer. Phew.

Maybe I believed being wrong or incompetent makes you naughty and I communicated that to him? I am wrong a lot, but I no longer think that it makes me naughty. Remember, I have the right to make a mistake. I don't have to be perfect to be good.

I can only describe our trip back as triumphant. We tell family and friends we are happy in Malaysia and show them photos of our new house near the jungle in Batu Ferringhi. People ask what happened and I tell them openly and without shame.

I speak about it at length to a group of old friends. I describe the perils of burnout and how I overcame it. "What's next?" they ask. I tell them, jokingly, I want to become a rest consultant. I want to help people learn to rest and play and cut out the things that drag them down. I want to help people take rest seriously, especially in our modern culture.

"Why is it so important?" they ask. I share a Vince Lombardi quote. When he was asked why he conditioned his players so hard at Green Bay, Lombardi said, "Because fatigue makes cowards of us all."

I was wrong when I asked God not to make something good come of this. With the months of near-suicidal depression in the rearview mirror, I can now see that the best lessons came, mixed with pain, during that period of my life. I burgeoned my faith in God. I learned to love and appreciate what I had and what I was missing with my head buried in hundreds of emails and the shame of never being enough. I found a way to rest, to have fun again. I started owning the life God gave me; all of it.

No fatigue, no being a coward. Just "feel the fear and do it anyway."

Wednesday, August 2, 2006

We return to Malaysia on a very jagged, drawn-out flight schedule with many layovers and not enough sleep or water. Dave brilliantly arranges a stop at an airport hotel in Kuala Lumpur. We rest up so we can face the house full of boxes that are waiting to be unpacked at our new home. We plan to get busy to avoid the inevitable blues that will come from leaving our family and other loved ones in the US.

We have splurged and rented a house on the north end of Penang Island. There is a wide, panoramic view of the jungle covering the blue and green-hued mountains that create the island's backbone. The sea is a five-minute walk the other direction. Because the jungle is right across the street, we are visited regularly by black monkeys with white rings around their eyes, as well as the occasional huge monitor lizard. The house has a stucco and wood frame, an outdoor living room with ceiling fans, a teak dining table, and bamboo couches with white cushioned chairs. We have the largest *garden* (Asia's elegant term for what we call a "yard") in the neighborhood, ready for badminton. Best of all, the house comes with a black dog named Lucy, who looks like a medium-sized Labrador.

We imagine a year of coffee mornings and sleepovers and Christmas parties. Joy, hope, and love consume us. We don't know it yet, but this inviting, two-story white stucco home with its red tile roof will be our home for the next three years.

We've returned to start a different kind of adventure. This is better than I imagined it. We aren't "wannabes" any longer.

I guess it takes what it takes.

Chapter 20
A LETTER TO MYSELF

In November of 2006, while settling into our house in the resort town of Batu Ferringhi on Penang's northern end, I began a job as a sales manager for an inductor manufacturer. I made the connection for the interview with an inviting, friendly woman I met at the International Women's Association. This job was perfect for me, and mostly consisted of speaking with and answering emails from Americans during my customer's business hours. I desperately wanted to break up with the patterns and habits that made my work stress deadly, and I achieved my goal. I found a job I could enjoy.

Our final three years in Malaysia were filled with incredible memories. God provided friends, growth, joy, and life. I volunteered at the Youth with a Mission (YWAM) program and helped women who had been sex trafficked. I became a leader at the Penang International Church. Sean excelled in school and was given the privilege of learning from the incredible teachers in the Penang International School primary program. Ms. Rajamoney, Ms. McDonald, Ms.

Kaur, and Mr. Westall... I am forever in your debt.

In 2009, we moved home to the US—first to St. Petersburg, Florida, then to Louisville, Kentucky. Like many people with the "hero" mentality, I wanted to help others. I wanted to help people remove depression and fear from their lives, so I had to develop the knowledge and skills to do that. I also wanted to figure out exactly what happened to me in Penang.

In 2011, I went back to grad school to study counseling psychology. Doing this as a way to understand depression was such a "try hard" thing to do. While reading a Brené Brown book like *The Gifts of Imperfection* was eye-opening, it evidently wasn't enough for me! I felt if I could understand it, maybe I could avoid it and help others do the same.

In 2013, I obtained my master's and wondered where I could contribute. How could I help someone else avoid what happened to me? Or, if it had already happened to them, how can I help them heal?

At first, I helped at several agencies, working with people whose chaotic childhood had spilled into adulthood. I learned so much while going on their journey with them: fear, conflict, confusion, and the feeling of being out of control. I worked to help people battle pain, anxiety, depression, childhood trauma, and addiction. I felt like I was a child trauma specialist and my clients were 40 years old.

By 2018, I noticed that many of the people I counselled had physical and relational symptoms related to work stress. They assumed these were a normal part of life. Just as I had, they had encountered painful things. Like me, their unmanageable work stress and illness forced them to leave good situations and people they loved. I wanted to help others avoid having to go through that.

I realized I had a chance to help clients in a unique way. So, I started a practice called Work Stress Guru. I have made myself available for when my clients decide it's time to address the symptoms of panic, anxiety, and burnout. When these things threaten my client's health and get in the way of earning their livelihood, we work to set things right.

I sit in awe of the change that I see, their resilience and strength. I have a front row seat, and I get to watch people transform from a place of suffering and depression to freedom and emotional wealth. It's at these times that I know I'm doing what I was meant to do.

Recently, I began thinking about something that's been nagging at the back of my mind for years.

If I could go back to 2005, during the lowest point of my burnout, and have a talk with myself, what advice would I offer? What words would have penetrated my broken heart and my defensive bulwark? What would have helped me heal, or at least put me on the path?

If I could write a letter to myself, with 15 years of hindsight, here is the letter that I imagine sending:

Letter to Myself after 15 Years of Experience

Dear Janna,

First, if someone loved you before you made this huge mistake, they'll love you afterward. And the opposite is also true. Those who did not like you before you made your huge mistake, won't care afterward. In the most important areas of your life—love and loyalty—not much has changed. Be loved. Open up the trap door to the basement of your broken heart and be loved.

Second, don't argue with everyone who tries to help you. Don't fight off others' attempts to show you reality. Trust someone else and stop blocking their advice. If you receive a piece of advice that you hate, learn why you hate it. While you shouldn't take all the blame, be humble enough to ask, "How did I participate?"

Third, experience favor, kindness, and grace from God—even when you disappoint! No, *especially* when you disappoint. You may feel like you're "cheating" if you need God's grace or other people's help, but that's just not the case. If you look around and wonder how relaxed, unruffled husbands and workmates avoid being used and burnt out, don't envy them...*copy them!*

Fourth, there is no magic formula. But if there was one, it would be what your Gran said when you went off to college: "Be your own best friend." Keep getting rest, even if it's awkward when you try. Heal your body and your heart; your brain will follow. Stop pedaling twice as hard to be liked half as much. Focus on what's important and say no to what's not. Boundaries are a single-player game.

Fifth, realize that something good came from your stretches of exhaustion. Consider this: it forced you to rest. It was the only time you told people to leave you alone and stop asking you to do something. It was the only time the light on the top of your taxi flashed "Off Duty," and you were relieved to not pick up any fares.

Sixth, you had some help getting this way. The origin of your guilt, fear, and shame are hard for you to see. The contempt and chaos you experienced when you were a child means you haven't grown up all the way, painful as that is to admit. When adults didn't always act like adults, you worried sick about them. You grew accustomed to feeling sad and frustrated as you tried to help them "get better." Let go of this and you won't be so tired.

Finally, just because you follow God doesn't mean you won't experience heartache. It also doesn't mean you get to tell Him how everything is supposed to go. No need to be the General Manager of the Universe. And you don't have to make it all right for everyone. Grow up, be grateful, and focus on the next right thing you need to do. You may think this will be the end of you. It will actually be the beginning.

Love, Janna

THE SECRETS TO THRIVING: LIES, HABITS, AND CHANGES

There are many resources, including books, podcasts, and videos, that explain solutions for anxiety, depression, and burnout. Mindfulness and meditation, for example, are easy, if not awkward, practices to learn and they are proven to help bring calm even to soldiers with severe PTSD. Eating right, exercise, and getting rest are the bedrock of mental health, not just clichés.

All these things help calm the lightning storm inside our skulls! They are the beginning of our efforts to protect our mental health.

But I want to do more than fix physical symptoms or act as an HR consultant and propose new programs at work.

What I most want to do is help people achieve *long-term change*. I've asked myself, "Is there some way to get at the root of panic events, long-term anxiety, burnout, and depression before they ever begin? Is there a way to offer permanent change in how people think about themselves, their work, and how they handle their closest relationships?"

In my case, I needed to reorder thoughts and process emotions in order to get better. I had to question the assumptions that dictated my actions and my life's habits.

One of the oldest truths in counselling is that the counselor is a wounded healer. We are struggling with mental illness and should be getting better. Since I never wanted to be a hypocrite or prescribe something I was not willing to do, I took a long and hard look at myself. I found that my assumptions and habits played a significant role in my ongoing anxiety, depression, and eventual burnout. I was blind to them. But as I learned more about myself and others, they became more apparent.

I take these assumptions and habits very seriously because I feel they almost killed me.

So, what follows is a description of:

My Lies (or Assumptions)
My Habits
What I Did to Change (and what you can do too!)

Lies I Believed:
Assumptions That Lead to Burnout

The following is a list of assumptions I made about work stress, about others, and about myself. These assumptions motivated me to maintain my work stress habits. They are the fastest way to sum up what I and others believe in our core. They are the thoughts we automatically think, without noticing.

- Others are shocked and wonder how I got this position.
- People who rest are lazy.
- Having work piled on me is love.
- I do everyone a favor when I stress at work.
- The problems at work are unchangeable.
- My leaders don't want to help me, even if they could.
- My work stress is someone else's fault.

Most of these assumptions are held by people like me who have a "hero" mentality. To be clear, being a "hero" in the workplace is *not* necessarily a good thing. Your boss might love it, but your personal life and mental health often take a beating as a result.

Where does this term stem from? One model counselors use to understand chaotic situations is called the Karpman Triangle (or Drama Triangle) first proposed by Stephen Karpman, M.D. It's called a Drama Triangle because, in chaotic situations, people can play one or all of the three different roles: "Hero," "Villain," or "Victim."

People naturally go about life filling the role in which they are most comfortable. Some people are genuinely heroic and overly concerned about others. They act like Heroes most of the time. Some people are often asked to do the dirty work, to say 'no' or deliver bad news. They play the role of Villain. Others have truly been hurt or disadvantaged by life. They often engage with the world as Victims. People can play any of these roles in any given situation.

"Villain" is in quotes because people who say "no" are not always the bad guy/gal. "Victim" is in quotes because people can blame others even if they have not experienced legitimate betrayal or abuse. And "Hero" is in quotes because not every person who rescues others or provides care is as angelic as they appear. For example, Heroes can, at times, exhibit an unattractive combination of self-righteousness and resentment when their image or heroic reputation is in danger.

When we become rigidly stuck in one of these roles, we assume others are playing the opposing roles and we treat them accordingly. In the context of my own story, I felt my bosses were the Villains, that my employees were the Victims, and that I needed to assume the Hero role and take the whole world on all by myself.

Well, how did that work out?

When we interact with others in this limited way, basing our emotions and thoughts on stereotypes and melodrama, it is terrible for relationship dynamics. The outcome, whether at work or home, suffers.

Assumptions made by work stressed people sound a lot like those of "Heroes" and a little bit like those of "Victims."

However, to keep it simple, I refer to consistently burnt-out people as "work stress heroes."

Let's examine some of these work stress hero assumptions in a little more depth:

1. "Others are shocked and wonder how I got this position."

Many of us have energy, great ideas, and passion. We are very capable and smart, yet we are a little anxious that we cannot fill the shoes we've stepped into. We feel we've reached up to a position of great responsibility and importance and hope we look the part we are playing. We are going through something called "Imposter Syndrome."

In this overpowering assumption, a hero thinks, 'I don't belong here.' Many of our secret thoughts and emotions swirl around it. This assumption is so strong and ingrained that we make daily decisions and take actions because of it. We rarely notice until it's pointed out.

The motivation to play the "Imposter" varies by person. We secretly wonder how we—a 55-year-old man living in an apartment; an obese woman with two dependent children; a 35-year-old who can't live up to his father's achievements; a female in a male-dominated field—could have possibly gotten this position. How did we trick them? How can they not see what we see?

Many coaches call this a 'self-limiting belief.' In addiction recovery it is called 'terminal uniqueness.' To us heroes, however, it doesn't matter what they call it. Even if we understand it, we also understand that it is a stressor that makes us work harder. And if we work harder, even to the point of burnout, we can achieve things that no one, including ourselves, would have thought possible.

2. "People who rest are lazy."

We assume most people have been taught a good work ethic and were raised by hard-working people. One of the best things a teammate can say about us, in any setting, is, "He works hard." From childhood, we are praised for our level of work. We win 'Strong Contributor' awards regularly. We joke, "I'll sleep when I'm dead."

So, people who rest, we reason, are lazy.

As a natural extension to that, people who say 'no' are lazy. In our opinion, our organization has enough negative people who consistently say no. We like being the person who says 'yes.' When heroes are stressed to the point of burnout, this mentality keeps us in the storm. We don't want to feel like we're lazy, too. We might be encouraged to question this assumption by a good friend or coach, but we don't even have the time to truly examine our thoughts. We're far too busy for that.

So, even though our mind and body are screaming for rest, we don't trust it.

Why do we not trust that rest gets results? Because work stress heroes don't think this advice applies to us. We are in the trenches, and we accept that being overworked is normal for us. We think doing less is a frightfully stupid strategy. We believe that more hard work is the answer because that's what got us this far.

We tell ourselves that doing less would be a lazy look. It would only cause us *more* anxiety, not less.

3. "Having work piled on me is love."

This assumption is so cliché it goes unnoticed and unchallenged. Work stress heroes like us often feel that having our emails full of requests and our desks covered in projects equals love. Becoming a subject matter expert or area head requires us to work on high profile projects. Job security and chances for leadership are the reward.

Extra work brings all the things that make for great jobs: praise, recognition, results, meaning, and connection. We volunteer for a high workload because it feels great to be engaged, and we want the respect of our teammates. It fuels camaraderie and solidarity in the workplace, even though you go home and can't connect with your loved ones. Even though you can't get a good night's sleep.

For those who care a great deal about their work and consider it a calling, these things provide meaning and purpose. So, we don't think that leaders trusting us with workloads that more than double other colleagues' is a bad thing. We assume more work means more love.

But overwhelm and burnout are real.

Lots of work is good, until it's not.

4. "I do everyone a favor when I stress at work."

Work stress heroes like us clean up everyone else's messes, and we worry where the next mess is coming from. We think, 'When I *don't* worry, *that's* when everything goes wrong.' In this way, we believe we're doing everyone a favor when we stress at work. So, why would we try to reduce our stress?

Our bosses and supervisors are aware that they get

greater production out of us in the short term because we're stressed. If we heroes willingly sign up to do more work with less resources, few people will stop us. Even after a company meeting when execs and owners talk about maintaining a work-life balance and practicing self-care, we keep on playing the hero, because we know that *they* know that's our role in the company.

So, our boss, division, and company assume we're fine being stressed. They reason that heroes like the hard-charging, take-no-prisoners culture and figure out the best way to survive in it, because it's mostly true.

5. "The problems at work are unchangeable."

We don't see how our work culture could possibly change. We proceed with the underlying thought that the problems we face are too big and unchangeable. There's no more staff being hired, and we have an uninformed leader that will never change. So, like Don Quixote, we continue to tilt at windmills with a deep-seated belief that we must make do with what we have and big solutions will never be implemented.

6. "My leaders don't want to help me, even if they could."

Many heroes are knee deep in mission-critical projects, cases, and infrastructure decisions. We are dealing with huge, million-dollar-a-day issues. But we cannot get time on our boss' calendar to talk.

In this vacuum, we assume, 'This problem is my problem to solve alone. No one above me has time to talk to me about it, let alone stop and help me with this huge concern.'

If we do get to talk with leadership about our concerns, we end up answering questions instead. Furthermore, we heroes feel we are not allowed to disagree or ask questions of our own.

We don't want to argue with leaders. We don't want to come off as the desperate person who can't get along with management. So, because we won't barge in, we are denied valuable facetime with our leaders. As a result, decisions are made for our team without our input. We conclude that leaders don't understand our problems.

The ball rolling downhill picks up steam, and the less time we have to collaborate with leaders, the more we begin to assume that leaders do not want to help. We think it's not that the leaders don't have the ability. It's that they don't have the *desire*. This belief makes us much less likely to do the things that would likely relieve some stress in the team environment. We collaborate less, stop advocating for our team, and then give up trying to elicit better decisions from above.

7. "My work stress is someone else's fault."

Many different circumstances sustain our heroic work stress. We blame outside forces for our burnout: leaders, our company's culture, co-workers, the markets, and even world events. We assume that the cause of our work stress and burnout exists almost entirely outside ourselves.

Not getting the focus, direction, training, praise, time, career development, or human concern we need from leaders causes us stress. We look around at problems that seem permanent and unchangeable, and we think, 'Everything and everyone adds to my stress. Nothing and no one ever takes it away.'

Even if all of these issues improve, even if our bosses are open-minded, ethical, curious people who focus and prioritize, we often still have trouble with work stress. Leaders and colleagues can show up for us, listen, and give ample attention and collaboration, but we still struggle with burnout because we assume that it only comes from others. Therefore, it can only be solved by others.

My Habits that Keep Work Stress Going

In addition to assumptions, many of our habits keep work stress going. They keep us hard at work and burnt out. Let's talk about seven of these:

- Taking on 2x-10x workloads
- Catching every ball thrown
- Constant feeling of "never enough"
- Trying to delegate, but not being able to
- Unhealthy stress in every job worked
- Hiding the fact that we are overwhelmed
- Expecting too much from work

1. Taking on 2x-10x workloads

There is a saying among veteran managers: "If you want something done, give it to a busy person."

This is wise advice in the short-term. Heroes are the busy, stressed people who do more work than our co-workers. We work on 50 cases while our colleagues each work on 10. Doing more than our fair share is usually not unique or noteworthy for work stress heroes. It's something we've come to expect.

For this greater amount of work, heroes often receive recognition, raises, and promotions. They lift the bar. The ball is in the hands of the most capable athlete and our companies seem to benefit from better results. But inevitably, we heroes begin to feel used and exhausted.

A hero's teammates can begin to build resentments. They want a chance to grow and develop too, so they move to another company, leaving behind recruitment, retention, and engagement headaches for everyone up and down the ladder.

The habits of others add to the problem. Most business training focuses on ways to deal with teammates who play "Victim" and "Villain" to the detriment of the team. Trainers rarely focus on the negative consequences of a colleague's "Hero" mentality. Instead, they praise heroes for perfectionism, attention to detail, and individual effort. Leaders turn a blind eye to the hero's lack of collaboration and unwillingness to spread around the work, while laying on the praise and providing them chances at career development. So, while this habit works to get things done in the short term, burnout and colleague resentment is never far in the horizon for the hero.

2. Catching every ball thrown

My son's football coach gave this advice each day before practice. "Don't let anyone outwork you. Catch every ball they throw." Never mind that my son played on defense—saying "yes" and catching every ball gets us what we want. We become energized. There's a rhythm to it. There's a dopamine rush. It doesn't irritate us. It settles us!

Catching every ball thrown feels natural, because it's what heroes are made for. It matches our energy output with our need to be active.

However, as we age and our responsibilities grow, catching every ball is an automatic habit that keeps heroes stressed and on edge. Just as uneven distribution of projects creates problems, catching everything leaves little time for focus and prioritization.

It's also very hard on the morale of the tired people who work for a hero. They are the unwilling Victims when they cannot say no to the hero above. They too must catch all the balls thrown.

3. Constant feeling of "never enough"

With all this extra work and our need for perfection, it is ironic that work stress heroes have a common refrain: "I just feel like what I'm doing is never enough. I have this thought a million times a day. I wake up in the middle of the night with that feeling." We are plagued with the thought that we can and should be doing more.

We can have a win—the completion of a project or the conclusion of a successful year—but we don't take time to enjoy it. It seems as if, during the moments after a win, we see what others have achieved and the air goes out of our sails. We'll hear from an angry leader about the one thing we forgot, and we ruminate about that instead of the 200 things we did right. And, just like that, we stop enjoying our recent success.

We cannot conquer the feeling that what we do is never enough. We go back to worrying and grinding.

4. Delegation doesn't seem to work

As we grow in our jobs, we are asked to move from being sole contributors to leaders. In order to become managers, franchisees, directors, vice presidents, and executives, we must prepare for our first giant leap.

We must become examples of how it's done. Sales professionals become sales managers. Registered nurses become charge nurses. Star managers run several locations. We must multiply our singular productivity by leading a team of individuals so they can be as productive as we have been.

Work stress heroes find the delegation part of this process very difficult. We have been raised to roll up our sleeves, to fight for the person beside us, and to never ask of others what we would not ask of ourselves. No wonder it's so confusing for us when we're told we must delegate and manage the people on our team, and not *do* the actual work that needs to be done.

Even when we find the will to truly delegate, team members seem to disappoint us, screw things up, and generally create more work for us heroes. So, after not giving it much time, we abandon our experiment with delegation and go back to covering for those who can't or "don't want to" do the work.

5. Unhealthy stress in every job worked

We may be buoyed by the thought of a new position in a new firm, going out on our own, or changing careers completely. We might even entertain escape fantasies of delivering pizza at a beach resort.

We start new jobs wanting to turn over a new work/life balance leaf. But we also feel the pressure to show everyone how capable and hard-working we are. So, for the first 3 months, we go back to our old work stress hero habits and set everyone's expectations about our capacity and willingness to do more with less. We kid ourselves that it is just to make a good first impression, but we've inevitably painted ourselves into the same old corner.

Consequently, no matter where we work, we find unhealthy work stress awaiting us. Old hero habits, as well as old conflicts and resentments, return, deflating our newfound confidence and making us ask the question, "Why am I like this?"

Critical or co-workers who work fewer hours will always agitate and irritate us. When those in authority do not notice our talent, knowledge, and contributions, this triggers us. We detach and wonder why we've chosen another "loser" team. We eventually notice how different we are from others who worry less. We become envious of those who do not take on as much work stress. The sad cycle is complete.

6. Hiding the fact we are overwhelmed

If you've ever tried to achieve something, even as inconsequential as singing in the 8th grade talent show, you've heard the advice, "Fake it till you make it!" Another phrase along these lines goes, "What you lack in competence, make up for in confidence."

This is, as many have discovered, very good advice for getting over the jitters, letting go of self-limiting beliefs, and ignoring the people who said we'd never amount to anything. When people face adversity and persevere, of course that's good. When people play hurt and keep going, it's a success story worth celebrating.

So, we don't let others see us shake, and we don't display our weaknesses for just anyone. Not until the challenge has been met and we've won.

But as heroes, we take this habit a few steps further. We are well versed at hiding our fear and exhaustion. We have lots of practice at hiding the fact that we are overwhelmed and in pain. We put on a strong face.

We are the proverbial frog who hopped into the water when it was still cool. But home life, work circumstances, and world events turn the water so hot that it begins to boil, and the hero does not know how to turn down the heat. We've gone way past the point of asking for help or demanding a change in systems. We've waited too late to wave our hand for help. The result?

Burnout, divorce, quitting, or being fired.

7. Expecting too much from work

All these tendencies are made more intense by one hero habit: Expecting too much out of work. Because work holds so much identity, meaning, and value for us, we get a lot out of it when it's going well, and we expect more out of it when it's not. We care *so much* about what others at work think of us perhaps because we've invested there and neglected other areas of our lives. Our loved ones are left to scratch their heads and wonder why.

We get confidence, approval, camaraderie, and a place to hide when other parts of our lives don't go as planned. We get a chance to prove that we have worth. Add all this to the fact that many heroes are highly paid, and you can see why we are super-sensitive about what goes on at work.

What I did to Change: Questioned All Assumptions, Got Some Different Habits

If these assumptions and habits keep you stressed, is there any way out? Are there real, effective solutions?

Yes, solutions exist.

There are steps I took to understand myself, to decide what I would and wouldn't do. I established some *new* habits and changed the way I worked. I rediscovered the courage I once had and focused on what mattered most both at work and at home. I found an entirely new way to interact with others. This is what worked for *me*. I hope some of them work for you.

It seemed awkward at first, but I invested in these new and profoundly world-changing habits:

- Checked My Blind Spot
- Experimented with "No"
- Let Others Contribute
- Found Focus, Not Fear
- Prevented Panic
- Invested in Rest
- Went Where I was Celebrated, Not Just Tolerated

1. I Checked My Blind Spot

I didn't just agonize over the question, "Why am I like this?"

I experimented on myself, and I took the time to actually find the answer.

After I quit and was humbled by my situation in Penang, I went deeper and figured out what kept me grinding even after I was burnt out and exhausted. I thought about why I chose work over those I love, and I came to understand how I developed my stress-inducing habits and assumptions.

I realized that the most important person responsible for reducing my amount of work stress is me. If I continued to blame everyone else, I never would have understood that, all along, I had the power to change.

Over the years, I realized how difficult, long-forgotten events played a part in the decisions I made. I had overcome adversity and lived to tell about it, so I said, "Hey, what didn't kill me made me stronger!"

These accumulated events "assigned" me the role of Hero: fighting against Villains, and rescuing Victims. However, Victims and Villains are not the only ones playing games. Myself, and heroes like me, also participate in the dysfunction of the Drama Game.

I also learned that being a workaholic is a common trait among adult children of alcoholics/addicts.

Could any of these issues be hidden in your blind spot too?

I encouraged the lopsided distribution of work and denied others the chance for praise. I hogged the limelight and then, when the going got tough, I harbored resentments and felt exhausted and unappreciated. I noticed the perils of playing the hero role in Malaysia but didn't act upon it even as my life was falling apart around me. Today, I have the benefit of hindsight, but *you* can act before it's too late.

In time, I figured myself out, found my tendencies, and saw how the past contributed. Books on codependency, boundaries, and addiction helped me when I was humble enough to learn. Also, I talked to a counselor, a mentor, and a spiritual advisor, as well as my husband, Mom, and best friend. I experienced their compassion and braced myself to hear things I didn't want to hear.

My advice: Brace yourself and check your blind spot. A great book for this is by Henry Cloud and John Townsend called *Boundaries: When to Say Yes, How to Say No to Take Control of Your Life.*

In checking my blind spot, these resources were also helpful:

- www.adultchild.org
- https://www.acesconnection.com/blog/got-your-ace-resilience-scores
- https://www.boundariesbooks.com/pages/quiz
- https://www.psychologytoday.com/us/blog/fixing-families/201106/the-relationship-triangle

2. I Experimented with "No"

This is a big one.

"No" is a very powerful word in business discussions. Warren Buffet and Bill Gates both highly recommend that it should be our default answer.

For decades, successful coaches, billionaires, doctors, and researchers who've studied work stress have advised everyone to work smarter and not harder. They explain and quantify the diminishing returns from over-work and over-worry. Again and again, they explain the impact with valid research results, even telling us work stress is more dangerous than second-hand smoke.

Since I regularly left meetings with most of the action items on my personal to-do list, this advice was spot on. Saying no helped with that.

However, meetings aren't where I began. Experimenting with no helped me climb onto a plateau of safety—a place to regain my footing, my health, and my mojo. I needed a place to rest and heal up, like a soldier who'd just been in a hell of a fight. So, I began with saying no in small ways. If someone asked, "Do you have a minute?" I'd say, "Actually, I don't this week," with a smile on my face.

At one point in my life, the thought of doing this seemed impossible; it gave me a stomachache. But I considered this: I did not have to change completely, or all at once, in my use of the word "no." I needed to develop the good habit, and this took time.

Cloud and Townsend, co-authors of *Boundaries*, suggested that while I was learning to set boundaries at work and at home, I work for six months on building a simple habit of saying no. I was supposed to make it my default. There wasn't any real risk either! I could always go back and say yes in most cases, but what this early exercise taught me was how much I automatically said "yes." It was powerful. *Life-changing.*

So, I experimented with no in the smallest of ways— things like bathroom breaks, leaving at the same time each day, taking time to eat a nutritious meal more often than not. These were basic human needs that I did not protect because no was not a habit for me.

During this time, I was tempted to provide an

explanation. I tried not to. If I couldn't say "no" without adding an explanation, I'd tell them, "I'm on a deadline." If they pressed further, I'd ask them, "Does our conversation have anything to do with my major deadline?" I had previously assumed it would take less time to just have the short conversation and do the task. But that was 100% not true since I usually left most conversations with the majority of the to-do items. Saying "not now" helped minimize the work that people would lob over the fence at me.

Saying "no" because I needed to pay more attention to my personal life proved a bit harder. But I pushed through the awkwardness, and the results were staggering. I saw that attending to my personal life and that of my loved ones sustained my energy level. And energized employees are what companies need.

I was tele-commuting in my second job in Malaysia. I'd go offline to eat lunch with my husband or go to my son's baseball game and stop responding to emails/meeting invites at my regular shut down time. When I worked in-person in subsequent jobs, I resisted the urge to "sneak out." If someone approached me as I was about to shut down, I'd tell them, "I have to do something for my family." What was that something? I needed to be home to eat dinner with my husband and son.

After I experimented with saying "no" to colleagues and team members, I moved to a more important use of no. I said "no" to my own leaders and executives who wanted my attention for lower priority projects. Most companies and divisions make everyone aware of the highest profile projects. If deadlines were looming and I got invited to a meeting that was not focused on a high-profile project, I'd skip the meeting to see what would happen. Before, I had been too much of a goody-two-shoes to do that. But I let go of what others thought, said "no," and spent that time working on the important deadline that was looming over me.

If I didn't feel comfortable saying "no," I'd go to the person who set my strategic priorities. I'd beg off attendance at the meeting and ask them to ward off that request for me at a higher level.

Most shocking of all? My answers of "no" and "not now" resulted in *non-events.* There was not as much blowback as I predicted. Besides some frustrated leaders, there was no negative outcome 95% of the time and I was a more productive and healthier person as a result. My experiment proved to me that the world did not end when I said "no."

My advice: Resist the urge to blurt out the word "yes." Experiment with no. Most likely you'll have come to this realization for yourself. Perhaps it happened when a creative person got promoted ahead of you because they took time to think and collaborate. Perhaps it happened when work stress forced you to take a leave of absence.

If you have any doubt that the time to say "no" is now, please read a book published in 2013 by Dr. David Posen entitled *Is Work Killing You? A Doctor's Prescription for Treating Workplace Stress.*

Now is the time to start saying NO.

3. I Let Others Contribute

After years in business, I became so entrenched in the habit of doing things myself that I preferred it. When I complained to teammates or family about the amount of work on my plate, they'd usually make the dreaded suggestion, "Ask for help! Get someone else on your team to do it. At least part of it."

However, instead of planning a way to offload some work and get some relief, I'd get even more frustrated. I predicted bad outcomes at the thought of someone else helping me. 'They are not as fast, accurate, or talented as I need them to be,' was my arrogant and inaccurate thought. I simply thought they wouldn't do the job as well as I could do it.

I have been told that I developed this bias because I grew up being a "little adult." My foolish assumption was that others don't measure up and can't. So, picking up their slack naturally fell to me.

This is how I developed a "Me" program. But how long could I sustain it? How long could I keep going until the workload mismatch hurt my physical and mental health? Also, if I asked for all the important work, how did my teammates feel? How could they be valued enough to stick around? How long before the end product of the whole team suffered?

I had to turn work and life into a "We" program. Examples abound of stars finally winning the championship because they trusted a fellow player. Brady needed receivers and Jordan needed a 3-point shooter! I was never a Brady or a Jordan, but if you are, pay attention. There are so many success stories and TED Talks that demonstrate the necessity of input from everyone.

Long-term success is sustained when people learn to work together instead of just one person playing the hero. My favorite explanation of this comes from CEO Margaret Heffernan's TED Talk called, "Why it's Time to Forget the

Pecking Order at Work."

When I stopped playing God in my silo, complaining that I was the only one working late, others were more open to collaborate with me.

I made the effort to be more in sync with others at work and at home, not just a lone ranger. I asked my Higher Power for help, and I saw all the help that had already been provided. I was built to be surrounded by supportive people who are doing the work with me. I let go of the "Me" program where I was stuck being entitled and insecure.

My advice: Over time, build an incredible "We" program. Prove the African proverb: "If you want to go fast, go alone. If you want to go far, go together."

4. I Found Focus, not Fear

In performance reviews leaders would say, "You don't know how to prioritize," and I would resent it. They'd say, "You need to focus and say 'no' to the urgent, so you can say 'yes' to the important," and I would get angry.

Why? Because the person telling me to pay attention to priorities was also the one piling work on me. Being accused of lack of focus by a "slave driver" is infuriating. I'm sure you know the feeling! In my case, I needed to learn to manage my emotions. More than that, I needed to push back when managers contradicted themselves.

I learned to feel my emotions, to manage them and get past them. I looked deeper into why I couldn't prioritize and why it bothered me so much for others to suggest it.

I realized there were several reasons I couldn't prioritize:

- I didn't trust their strategy
- I didn't trust how the work was being distributed
- I didn't trust that leaders saw what was truly going on

I needed to trust my leader's strategic thinking, but didn't. I devoted time and energy to noncritical odds and ends just in case their strategy did not work. Because of my fear, I focused on things that had nothing to do with my leader's bigger strategy.

Moreover, experiencing FOMO (Fear of Missing Out) really piled on the workload. I feared that if I focused only on those tasks given to me, I would not get to work on high-profile projects, get recognized, and move up. I took on more instead of trusting the leaders who distributed projects.

But that wasn't all! I would back up or make up for others, and I made it my mission to keep projects rolling forward, even if I was never directly assigned them. In the back of my mind, I was afraid executives and leaders wouldn't realize what was going on and blame me when things went wrong. So, I took it *all* on my shoulders.

This had to change. I had to trust other teams to do their jobs, and I had to focus on *my* area. It took time, but I got out of the habit of hiding problems from leadership, especially when they weren't my own. I focused on my priorities, and if I or others didn't produce, then changes would have to happen. I started asking hard questions.

I took responsibility for my lack of focus. I figured out my values and what I could and should be doing with my talent, training, and desires. I made the hard decisions to get what I wanted, and when I did that, I naturally became more focused. As esoteric as that might sound, these were my first steps to living a life focused on what truly matters, both at work and at home.

I accepted that my executives were busy and burnt out too. Most of them genuinely wanted to help. I managed the negative self-talk, stopped assuming bad intent, and saw all the resources my companies and leaders had provided. I learned when to appreciate my autonomy and when to get time on my leader's schedule.

My advice: To truly focus on any endeavor, harness your emotions, know your desires and strengths, make the hard decisions, and have faith in your leaders and colleagues.

5. I Prevented Panic

For me, preventing panic became easier than dealing with panic once it started. Effective prevention involves a lot of the advice you'll get when you Google "How to prevent a panic attack." You probably know it by heart:

- Cut down on caffeine
- Exercise
- Get more sleep
- Pray (yes, it truly does help)
- Be mindful (stay in the now)
- Meditate (simple, silent, non-guided, emptying my mind of thoughts is enough)
- Practice acceptance
- Understand the difference between what is uncontrollable and controllable
- If it is severe, seek the help of a professional

I needed to put this advice into practice before panic and anxiety got out of hand. Just because I knew the tips, doesn't mean I was motivated to use them.

For example, I resisted meditation because I was too antsy. I knew little about the acceptance of other people's choices because I was too worried about helping everyone with their life. I was cynical about how much these positive habits would help.

Learning to use the tools required a level of self-encouragement I did not possess. I was too tired. When things got really bad, and the panic, anxiety, and stress mounted, it became almost impossible to take the advice. Still, it was painfully clear that preventing it with new habits was the only way forward, so I weighed the cost and benefit of all the advice and began doing some prevention.

One thing that helped with my motivation was to keep it simple. I chose just one thing that helped and focused on that. I would do that daily for six months or a year. If I missed a day, I'd just start again. Then, when I saw results from one, I would try adding another. I grew day by day and began to develop good, preventative habits.

I recommend the book *The Worry Trick* by Dr. David Carbonell. He outlines effective ways to treat severe phobias and decrease the length and severity of anxious periods. Read his book to see how he helps prevent panic and lessen the aftermath.

His (and my) advice: Start the day by lowering your baseline stress in the ways that work for you. When you encounter pain or difficulty, see the problem as uncomfortable and survivable, but not dangerous and deadly.

Ask yourself, "Is it unbearable or uncomfortable?"

6. I Invested in Rest, Unplugged

To beat work stress, I learned how to rest and unplug. Taking a break from work, but still thinking about work, is *not* rest. In order to unplug, you cannot be thinking about work when you are away from it.

I used to be a downer on vacation. I'd make my husband angry when I worked or checked emails on days off. Even getting a massage was annoying when my mind was racing with to-do list items. Honestly, it was worse than not getting a massage at all.

No matter my job, I failed to unplug because it was a difficult habit to break. So, for the longest time I observed that rest was a waste of time and money. Better to be back at work where there's a mountain of work waiting for me!

Unplugging is about leaving work worries, nervous checking, and constant thoughts at work where it belongs. To get better at it, I worked out the emotions and tendencies that made me addicted to work in the first place. I dealt with my "Hero" tendencies, planned for vacation backup, said no, delegated, and depended on others—all habits that you must develop if you ever hope to destress and develop a better work-life balance. This attitude soon spilled over to work. I began to mono-task and take daily breaks.

Previously, long periods of work without a break were part of what made work stressful. Going all day and all night produced adrenaline that glued me to work thoughts, and it made rest and unplugging difficult. It would take days to unwind from that constant input, so, naturally, I thought vacations were ineffective.

Resting my mind for even four minutes during the workday improved my creativity, awareness, and problem-solving. After work, I unplugged more easily when I built breaks into each workday, because my brain became wired for it. When I took breaks seriously, I began to enjoy them and looked forward to doing something enjoyable or spending time with those I love. I keep a small sign near my monitor that reads: "Breaks = Good Sleep."

When I found a way to let something else besides work capture my attention, I let go. It doesn't matter what that something is; it will find you once you unplug.

My advice: Don't try unplugging once and quit. Keep doing it until you see some benefits.

A book that can help with this is *Rewire the Anxious Brain: How to Use the Neuroscience of Fear to End Anxiety, Panic, and Worry* by Catherine Pittman and Elizabeth Karle. This is especially a great book for those of us who like to geek out on the brain!

7. I Went Where I was Celebrated, Not Just Tolerated

I tackled some important things when breaking my burnout habits—dark emotions about myself: shame and anger.

My insecurities were also a part of my problem. In some cases, I joined teams and dove into jobs feeling like I was lucky to be included. I excused understaffing or low pay because I wanted to be a team player. I set myself up for work stress.

Guilt and hesitance were part of my anxiety. Chaos in childhood or contempt in adulthood caused a lot of dark self-talk. Not only did I feel horrible, but I also felt *guilty* for feeling horrible. It's as if I assumed a good whooping would get me back in line. If I made a mistake, I tolerated myself but had few positive things to say.

I realized that hating myself and self-discipline are not the same thing. I used a combination of humility and confidence to change. The time had come for me to do more than tolerate myself. No one was going to do that for me. So, I no longer agreed to roles with lots of responsibility, but which lacked the authority to get the job done.

At home and at work, I celebrated that I was alive, that I had not taken my own life. I engaged in being truly grateful for all the capabilities I possessed. I let go of my maladaptive and unrealistic perfectionism. I addressed my issues before I lost myself, my health, or my loved ones.

I stopped making everything alright for everyone else. No more hiding and being fake to be loved. I didn't focus on finding blame. I just noticed what enormous good I had in my life and focused on the next thing I needed to do or understand.

My advice: Go where you are celebrated, not just tolerated.

This is a pithy and easy-to-administer piece of advice, but it resonates with so many who feel underappreciated. However, it comes with a caveat: see if you can find change in your current situation before making a rash decision to leave a job or a marriage.

Learn to stand up for yourself, get your needs met, and build trust. This is not some "touchy feely" advice that only over-feeling work heroes need to hear. Going where you trust people is good for business. Paul J. Zak wrote a book in 2017 called *Trust Factor: The Science of Creating High-Performance Companies.*

And if you want to see a system that combines successful business models with authentic trust and care between human beings, read the book *Everybody Matters: The Extraordinary Power of Caring for Your People Like Family* by Bob Chapman and Raj Sisodia.

Final Thoughts from the Heart

If you suffer from work stress and are hiding your pain, my heart goes out to you. Anxiety, stress, and depression are scary, and it often feels like these emotions are making all the decisions. Comparing yourself to others who are (or at least seem to be) calm, cool, and collected can also be a heavy weight to carry.

If you're a work stress hero and you need to take only one thing from this book, take this:

> **You had help becoming the way you are. While it is powerful to take responsibility for getting better, it is crucial to understand some contributing factors that were most likely out of your control when you were younger.**

If your thermostat was set to scorching hot by chaos or difficult events early on in your development, you are going to be more reactive than others to negative events, and you will perceive them as dangerous. Hardship, pain, or living with a family member who had mental health and/or substance issues can make you more aware, and even attracted to the negative, the chaotic, and the worst-case scenario. Don't get me wrong either—this is a "strength" that can help you withstand adversity, take care of others, or anticipate and avoid mistakes.

But overusing this strength can make you demand complete control and perfection from yourself and others. It may have wired you to avoid any bad thing happening, and this is a sure recipe for anxiety, stress, and fear.

You can't be perfect or perfectly in control. But you *can* find a way to humbly let go of this illusion.

One day, I realized that despair, distrust, and self-pity were over for me. To survive and live a full life with my son and husband, I had to find another way. I processed the big things that happened in my life. I found a way to tolerate my mistakes. I forgave everybody for everything. With help from so many different people, I checked old assumptions, tried new ways of working, and welcomed constant reminders that change was worth the effort. It was slow and gradual, but the end result was real and permanent.

I experienced love and forgiveness and gave it to everybody else. As for me, I needed God/Jesus/Spirit to help me with the crucial steps of coming back. I needed His intense kindness, love, and forgiveness.

You may not recognize a higher power per se, but please recognize the power that's around you and don't try to do this all alone. Search with all your heart for kindness, love, and forgiveness, and I believe you too can experience emotional health.

There is no one standing in your way, so please: be brave enough to give it a try.

If I could have one more minute of your time...

Thank you for reading *Burnout Diaries: How Work Stress Almost Killed Me*.

Book reviews are very helpful to authors and readers alike.

If you found anything moving, helpful, or worthwhile in this book, a short review on Amazon, Goodreads, Barnes & Noble, or wherever you purchased this title would be greatly appreciated! Reviews and referrals are the best way to get the word out to people who may find this book helpful. Thank you so much!

Connect with the Author

If you would like to connect with Janna Donovan, please do!

To invite her to help your organization's teams and individuals avoid and recover from burnout, please email.

If you'd like to engage in compassionate work stress coaching, please reach out.

Email: workstress.guru@gmail.com
Twitter: @Janna_Listens
You can also visit her website at www.workstress.guru

www.ingramcontent.com/pod-product-compliance
Lightning Source LLC
Chambersburg PA
CBHW020903080526
44589CB00011B/412